PRAISE FOR *INCLUSIONABLE*

"With honesty, courage, and heart, this book shows how every leader can unlock their own 'superpower' of making others feel valued and seen. As someone who has spent her career focused on engagement and retention, I found myself nodding, learning, and celebrating every page. This book is more than a guide; it's a movement toward workplaces where people truly belong. For anyone committed to engaging and retaining talent in today's workplace, this book is indispensable. It challenges, inspires, and equips leaders to step forward with courage and make inclusion a daily reality."

—Dr. Beverly Kaye, coauthor of *Love 'Em or Lose 'Em, Help Them Grow or Watch Them Go, Up Is Not the Only Way,* and *Hello Stay Interviews, Goodbye Talent Loss*

"In *Inclusionable*, Christine Barnes gives us a practical hands-on roadmap for helping leaders at all tiers of an organization to undertake behaviors that promote warm welcome, connection, safety, and inclusion on teams and inside their organization's cultural fabric. At an incredibly painful time for the DEI movement writ large, this book brings passion to the topic and hopeful pragmatism to how leaders can make daily choices that make a meaningful difference. I hope this book can support new momentum to the evolution of the workplace as a source of belonging and healing."

—Amy Elizabeth Fox, CEO, Mobius Executive Leadership

"*Inclusionable* provides a comprehensive and practical guide at a time in our world when it is most needed. Christine Barnes provides a strong evidence-based perspective coupled with an authentic and pragmatic set of lessons that both support and confront all of us who are committed to building heathy and enduring communities and organizations."

—Andrew Chandler, organizational
design and development leader

"*Inclusionable* goes beyond theory to deliver practical strategies for leaders who want to build belonging and accountability. At its core is a powerful reminder: Inclusion is about human-to-human connection, and caring, servant leaders are inherently inclusive. Authentic, insightful, and timely, this book will help leaders create workplaces where people feel respected, valued, and part of something bigger than themselves."

—Germain L. St-Denis, author of *Empowering
People Through Caring Leadership*

"Drawing from her doctoral research, years of consulting experience, and genuine personal reflection, Barnes creates a guide that feels both practical and inspiring . . . Rather than treating inclusion as a corporate checkbox or fleeting trend, Barnes reframes it as a sustainable advantage . . . *Inclusionable* stands out for its clarity and compassion."

—Portland Book Review

"With a formidable and empathetic voice, Dr. Barnes guides readers on a journey of self-discovery and team transformation. Weaving a rich collection of narratives from diverse leaders, she emphasizes the critical importance of belonging. Her stories are not just lessons—they are invitations to reflect, adapt, and lead with authenticity."

—Britta Stromeyer, author and book critic,
National Book Critics Circle

"*Inclusionable* illustrates the strategic benefits of leading as an agent of change. A thoughtful leadership guide."

—*Foreword* Clarion Reviews

INCLUSIONABLE

INCLUSIONABLE

TRANSFORM HOW
YOU LEAD
AND ELEVATE
YOUR TEAM'S
PERFORMANCE

CHRISTINE BARNES, EdD

GFB

GFB

Published by GFB™, Seattle
www.girlfridayproductions.com

Produced by Girl Friday Productions

Cover design: Greg Mortimer
Production editorial: Kylee Hayes
Project management: Kristin Duran

ISBN (paperback): 978-1-967510-16-0
ISBN (ebook): 978-1-967510-17-7

Library of Congress Control Number: 2025917424

First edition

My book is dedicated to my parents, Ida and Cory, who tried to instill many values in me growing up. Some of them actually stuck! Three have become my North Star. From both of them, I learned, "Take the initiative; don't wait for other people to do what needs to be done." From my mother, Ida, I learned to always act with kindness. As a bonus, I got her smile. My father, Cory, believed that a sense of humor would make almost anything better, resulting in a lifetime of us kids' endurance of "dad jokes." I thankfully forgot most of those jokes but retained the desire to spark laughter and joy in others. These values and others they lived by have shaped who I am today.

My book is also dedicated to leaders everywhere who try every day, often without guidance, support, or even good examples, to help their people be their best version of themselves. That you are even trying speaks volumes about your commitment and your courage.

You are my heroes.

CONTENTS

INTRODUCTION

Hidden Heroes

I love heroes. *Batman, Superman,* and *Wonder Woman* comics were my twelve-year-old self's favorites, each new issue's plastic cover crackling with promise. These characters, with their cool costumes, wry humor, and unique superpowers, were easy to love.

They always showed up when they were most needed and dispatched various villains with careless ease, after which they would gaze into the dark night or the bright sun, a light breeze fluttering their capes, as they contemplated keeping humanity safe for another day.

These heroes gave hope for a bright future. I wanted to be them, or at least a sidekick like Robin to Batman. Although Robin always seemed to be on the defensive and maybe whined a bit too much.

As an adult, I yearn for heroes at work to help with inevitable crises and give hope for a brighter future. But a workplace dress code is more likely to be khakis and polo shirts, not masks and capes. And "pow" or "zap" are not much help when the villains are disengagement, workplace burnout, or a relentless drive for results!

AN UNLIKELY HERO

Superpowers are often nuanced, as I learned from Ben. He became my hero, but it didn't start out that way.

Deep into my doctoral research on the inclusionary practices of leaders in biotechnology, which inspired this book, I was interviewing Ben. He was one of twelve leaders who volunteered to discuss their knowledge and motivation about the inclusion side of the "diversity and inclusion" equation in their organization.

From the opening moments of the interview, I knew Ben was different from the other volunteers. Research standards dictated that I ask him for permission to record our session and offer to send him a transcript afterward for his edits and approval to use his comments for my research. Instead of simply saying yes to my request, he bluntly replied, "You don't need to send me anything. I don't care what you use from our interview."

My own biases snapped to attention. "Typical middle-aged white male scientist conceit," I thought. "All he cares about are facts and results. He won't have anything juicy to share about making a workplace more inclusive. Probably has the warmth of a test tube. Not sure what I'm going to get from this interview." Still, I had him for forty-five minutes and would get what I could.

We cranked through the first few questions. He volleyed back clipped, matter-of-fact answers in a steady, if mundane, manner. I lobbed the next one. "Tell me about a time you became aware that you needed to shift your own behavior about inclusionary practices and what you did next."

His answer froze me in place. "I got feedback in our assessment tool that some employees didn't think I appreciated their work," he mused. Then he went quiet for a breath or two, his gaze unfocused in memory. "At first, I was hurt. Then I decided I would give two recognitions per week. And it's funny, because I thought it was going to be really artificial and that I would have to force myself to do this. Maybe even make stuff up to meet the goal."

I was silent, trying to give him time and not scare him off.

He continued, "And what I found was that was not the case at all. It just took a small amount of thinking about or reflecting on my week, and okay, who am I going to recognize?"

He went on to tell an equally powerful story about a time when he organized a ropes-course team-building event. But he never gave consideration to whether everyone on his team would be able to participate. One team member exceeded a weight limit set by the adventure company hosting the team. The employee simply did not show up that day.

"When I learned this," Ben explained, "I felt terrible as a leader. And that was a big lesson for me."

MY OWN BIG LESSON

Ben's reference to the ropes course sparked a buried memory in me: Long ago, I had been him. As a keen outdoor-activities person, I loved anything with even a bit of challenge, including rock climbing. When I had a chance to design and facilitate a two-day sales-leadership team meeting, I quickly arranged an outing at a local climbing gym for the group.

I thought I had been so careful—I had my debrief points ready for after the event, such as, "What was it like to have to trust the person belaying you?" and "How did you support each other during the challenging parts?" We got through that two-hour event unscathed, and no one went to the emergency room or needed first aid. No one raved about it, though, and no one referred to it again. I was disappointed. How could they not see what a *great* metaphor rock climbing is for how we interact as a team?

Now I realize how my relentlessly positive cheerleading glossed over any possibility that one or more of the team members might have had a physical limitation or a fear of heights. I used only my own framework of what was fun, interesting, or useful for the team of leaders. There was no opening for anyone to speak up about it, and I'm guessing that no one wanted to admit to their peers that they simply did not want to do it.

HEROES AMONG US

Back to Ben. With those few thoughts, this blunt leader revealed his superpower of self-reflection. He gave me hope that leaders can create environments where people feel seen, valued, and that they belong, reducing burnout and stress. The gift he gave me was helping me to see my own biases, not just in the moment but in the rearview mirror too. I had to go beyond the costume to see the hero.

As much as we might revere heroes, we also think of them as being not like us. Superpowers can be hidden or nuanced, and when visible, they can make the person displaying them look different. Labels are assigned. Consider the X-Men, who are treated as misfits. People often fear or dislike what is different, because they don't know how to interact with someone unlike them and instead seek out people they feel most comfortable with. One way that plays out in the workplace started with Title VII of the Civil Rights Act of 1964, which was created to end discrimination toward people who were different from the majority and to ensure all groups of people are accepted. Yet, even after six decades of companies and institutions trying to work within that law, discomfort with those who are "not like us" persists.

It often takes courage to share a unique opinion. Two colleagues once overheard me telling a manager that I thought a certain policy was stupid. Admittedly, it was not the most elegant or inspiring thing to say; I could have been more professional in empathizing with the manager while advising on the situation! When my peers reprimanded me sharply, telling me, "You can't say that. You have to follow the company policy," I felt unsafe about expressing my own views, separate from my team members, and that, to be accepted, I would need to either stop expressing myself or change my views. I now have a greater appreciation for anyone who is willing to speak up about something that needs to change, even if they are made to feel like a misfit.

A hero, in my opinion, does what they do in spite of being different and unappreciated. I wasn't thinking about heroes when I was working on my doctoral research and dissertation, but they emerged in my findings. That inspired me to write this book about inclusion, but not just about why it's a compelling strategy for leaders. I wanted to describe how leaders can authentically practice inclusion every day, engage employees, and improve business results.

But how do you start practicing inclusion when you don't know where to begin or what "good" looks like, especially when you haven't done it before or no one around you is doing anything? This is where courage comes in. My definition of "courage" in this book is action despite fear, not action without fear.

It can take a lot of courage, curiosity, and some helpful examples to become willing to be, look, think, feel, and act differently. You might be fighting a tide of indifference or people who question what you are doing. Just beginning is a heroic act, and I believe every leader has the potential to take this path. Inclusion is a superpower, and throughout this book, I'll show you how to find your version of it.

I want to tell you how I landed on the title of this book. It was harder than I thought it would be. Several times, I thought of a brilliant word or phrase and did a Google search. Each time, I was right—it was brilliant, so much so that someone else had gotten there before me. "Great minds think alike" is my consolation, as is including those terms in the chapter on tips, templates, and tool kits.

I kept interviewing people whose insights would help make my book one that people would actually want to read. The more people I spoke with and the more I shared my own passion for data, stories, and examples of what leaders can do, the clearer I got about the core of this book. I can sum it up in these words:

Inclusion + Able = Inclusionable

As in, if you are a leader, in title or intention, of a team, group, project, idea, or community, you are accountable for your people to be inclusive, and you are able to create an environment of inclusion. You might be surprised to hear this or may be skeptical or unimpressed. If it's this easy, why isn't everyone doing it? You might think it takes deep skill, training, or a superpower that only a few people have. Maybe you think that it should be someone else's job. If you're at least curious enough to read on, you are in the right place.

Both these words, "inclusion" and "able," are often misunderstood or misinterpreted. I want to clear things up.

I combined these two words because I want to show that they form a superpower that lies within leaders, untapped and dormant, until those very leaders believe they can access it.

I named this book *Inclusionable* because what has been done about diversity and inclusion up until now is insufficient, is never finished, and needs more people engaged in the daily routines of connection and relationships at work. To act requires a belief that we are able to create an environment of inclusion.

One difference in this book is that I center leaders as change agents—not human resources (also often referred to as HR), not the DEI team or department (also often referred to in various organizations as DE&I, D&I, and other iterations), not senior leaders, not the myriad external consultants who help shape the company, although you can probably count on these colleagues or professionals as allies. In my research, I asked questions meant to uncover what did or did not make a difference to leaders' effectiveness, based on what kind of knowledge they needed, what kind of motivation was present, and what kinds of organizational support were available.

As a leader, you, like those in my research, probably have pressure from above (usually from your boss, your senior leadership team, the board of directors, shareholders, or any combination of these) to contribute to the achievement of the company's goals.

You also have pressure from your employees, who look to you to set direction, strategy, expectations, goals, feedback, coaching, encouragement, career advice, and promotions, to name a few. This book aims to support you in your daily work and your everyday dealings within the system you are part of.

What you learn in this book may be especially beneficial if you work in or run a small(er) business and are resource constrained. The workshops, consulting, websites, tools, and coaching about hitting business targets may or may not be available, but you have a business to run. Your boss, your team, your customers, and especially your employees watch you and get information from you about what is important. Whether you like it or not, you are a role model for what counts.

Think of this book as what to do until the next psychological safety workshop comes along, or if you can't reach your DEI partner, or don't have one. Workshops, trainings, and coaches are critical, and yet the space or gap between your need and those things being available can be tough to fill. This book fills in those quiet or empty spaces where you know you need to act, or you want to do something but aren't sure of the best approach, where to start, or how you can influence your environment.

MY CONVERGENT PATHS

Every page of this book is based on the intersection of my expertise as an internal organization-development consultant, my training and passion as a coach, and my doctoral research on the inclusionary practices of leaders. I have observed, cajoled, consulted with, coached, and, yes, passed judgment on leaders at many levels, from new managers to seasoned senior executives in retail, publishing, and science, technology, engineering, and mathematics (STEM) companies. I write through the lens of the researcher, the observer, the participant, and sometimes as a leader who has had success and failure in that role.

I spent three years learning to write in an academic voice, and my dissertation is a testament to my success in doing so. That kind of writing seems insufficient for the kind of world you live in or the role you play. I want to interrupt your thinking, surprise you, make you laugh, and maybe even annoy you enough that you realize you can do some things differently and that you can't afford to wait until someone else comes along to do it for you or to tell you how to do it. To do all these things, I have had to pivot to a narrative voice while highlighting the best of my experience and learning from my two worlds of work and education.

Why now? Diversity, equity, and inclusion have been in the news for decades, but lately, we've seen examples of how partisanship, divisiveness, and conflict can grab headlines and obscure the reality of the daily work lives of most people in the United States. Most of these workers have a boss, and they are part of a team existing within a larger entity, which might have ten, a thousand, or a few hundred thousand other people.

I see you as someone who is leading a team, a department, a function, or an organization. You might have been in such a role for a while. Or maybe you are new to it or want to grow into it more. Maybe you want to improve business results or meet your goals, but you aren't sure what to do about that.

Your company might have resources that can help, such as a DEI team or an employee-relations group, or it might not. But even if you avail yourself of knowledge that will help, you may be unclear on how to apply or use those resources. Or you got some feedback yesterday and need help today. Or perhaps you just want to know that you are not alone, that you are still a good person trying to do your best, and that you can pick up practical tips in this book that will help you do something now, today, on your own, because often you are all that you have.

THE PATH OF THIS BOOK

Before I describe what is in this book, I want to be clear on what is *not* in this book.

There are few, if any, suggestions about diversity, diversity hiring, or diversity initiatives. The next chapter describes the diversity problem at a high level, but many, many other people have been working on solutions to the problem. I am not a diversity expert. I've never held that role, and I do not consider myself qualified to tell anyone what they should or shouldn't do about diversity in their organization, function, department, or team—which may sound strange in a book about inclusion.

But that's my point. This book is about how most of us have missed the boat when it comes to knowing what inclusion means at the most fundamental level of human-to-human interaction. We say "diversity-and-inclusion" like it's all one word, but we have little-to-no understanding that inclusion is the underutilized half of the DEI coin. Inclusion often gets overshadowed by diversity, especially because diversity is easier to track with metrics. Chapter one gives us the historical lens to understand why diversity initiatives overshadow work on inclusion: We've spent decades trying to get people through the door. What we've paid less attention to is whether they feel welcomed once they're inside.

We can't always get to inclusion through a workshop. Instead, we often need to address the environment. (There is nothing wrong with workshops. We need them, but too often we think the workshop will fix everything. Fixes will happen only if you, as a leader, understand how you shape and are shaped by the environment).

This book is a roadmap, connecting research, stories, and tips in ways that build upon one another. For example, in chapter one, I share how we got here, with the historical, legal, and societal context of the enduring challenge of diversity. This background includes the essentials we'll need for the journey of discovery we begin in chapter two, in which I share stories and research to make a case for the importance of self-awareness. To know yourself is to know your values, biases, and experience related to inclusion.

In chapter three, I explain how you can apply self-awareness to your role as a leader by knowing what your team, department, function, or organization needs from you. Knowing yourself and knowing your team are two layers of knowledge you need in order to move forward. In chapter four, I discuss the third layer, which is to know the organization or system within which you operate.

From there, we can examine the business problem you are trying to solve (or the opportunity you are trying to advance). Chapter five helps you diagnose your problem, which may sound simple but can be nuanced or complicated. Clarity about the problem you want to solve equips you to look for solutions.

Chapter six shares good inclusion practices of leaders, and chapter seven describes a framework for planning, doing, and then checking on the actions you set for yourself. I demonstrate how to check for and intentionally utilize tested and proven practices for inclusion, things you can try in your daily work.

Up to the end of chapter six, I focus on data and stories about inclusion to teach you important concepts, terms, and distinctions. This is foundational knowledge. I want to get you ready to make a shift, to take a specific direction at a crossroad on your journey.

Chapter seven gets into how to do what you need or want to do to become an inclusionable leader. I want to make it as easy as possible to take action, which is why I use a proven framework and suggested practices you can adapt to your needs.

Many people like me support leaders. Coaches, organization-development consultants (internal and external), organization-effectiveness professionals, change managers, project managers, and human-resources professionals all have a stake in the success of teams, departments, functions, and the organizations with which they work. In chapter eight, I outline the various ways you can tap into the network of support professionals around you during your journey of inclusion. You may not think of them as being involved in the topic of inclusion, but they can expand your thinking and multiply your success if you include them in your efforts. You might be surprised at how many partners you already have once you start thinking and talking about inclusion.

Chapter nine is about another kind of support for you as a leader: artificial intelligence, or AI. I share how AI is already impacting inclusion practices. If you are not yet interacting with AI on a variety of topics, you will be within the next six months. One of those topics will be how to be a more effective leader.

Chapter ten is both a summary of this book and a call to action. I use a quote about commitment to suggest actions you can take from each chapter. What will you do as a result of reading this book?

You can roam freely throughout this book. Chapter titles describe the topic or focus. If you want to skip past chapter two, "Know Yourself," because you believe you know yourself well, go right to chapter three and settle in. You can skip to the summary section at the back of each chapter: three key points, three reflective questions (which I always pose as "I" so you can hear your own voice asking the questions), and three actions to take (in which I always use "you," as these are suggestions from me to you that I hope you experiment with).

Maybe at some point, you will come back to chapter two and know yourself further, because as much as you might already know yourself, a reflection on "what do I know now that I did not know two, three, or five years ago?" could be very helpful.

I love to collaborate, and the resources section at the end of the book includes tools and templates I think you will find helpful. Everything here is something I have used myself, some for many years and others more recently discovered. Some are briefly mentioned in the chapters, while other resources are meant to round out your own tool kit. Pick and choose as you wish; I hope you enjoy them as much as I have.

Even though I am back in the business world where I belong, after writing and publishing academic-research papers, I've learned to give credit where it is due. The notes section at the end gives proper credit and citations for the various research, books, articles, and other sources of information I used.

Throughout this book, I promise to back up my suggestions or assertions with data (but not so much data that I put you to sleep), proving that I am not just stating my opinion but have also consulted a lot of smart and experienced people. And I promise to tell you a few stories about real people who are just like you. (All interviewees' names have been changed to honor privacy.) In telling these stories, I want to show how our journeys can take many directions and still include acts of bravery and inclusionable leadership.

It was my job as the collector of these stories to be faithful to the intention and uniqueness of each human telling their story. I had to be careful not to alter the stories with my own biases or assumptions. Over time, I realized I was a witness to people coming into themselves. Sometimes they questioned the status quo; more often they questioned themselves. They said, not quite in these words, "How I'm showing up at this moment is insufficient. I need to do something different."

From this place of questioning, the leaders, regardless of race, ethnicity, or whether they were consultants, employees, or from the United States, England, or Canada, all believed without fail that they were accountable for making a difference. To change something or someone, even if it's themselves, on the topic of inclusion in the workplace. As I heard their stories, I saw in them many everyday heroes. I was inspired by them, and I hope you are too. No cape required.

CHAPTER ONE

How Did We Get Here?

"How has it come to this—that so many people wear [metaphorical] masks at work? I can't see you as a full human if you wear this mask. And yet they want to be seen. When I tell my own story, sometimes they feel comfortable with me and drop their masks. But mostly people keep them on. Even I have to maintain mine at times. We are missing the boat."

We were on a Zoom call for an interview about my book. Charles, an executive at a global technology company, was challenging the status quo about work behavior, not me. Yet I felt the intensity of his only slightly rhetorical question. We were talking about inclusion in companies, and he wondered out loud at the ongoing struggle of companies and leaders to treat people as unique human beings.

In the introduction, I described leaders who quietly practice inclusion as heroes. Charles's story reminded me that many of those heroes wear metaphorical masks—guarding parts of themselves even while creating brave spaces for others. It takes ongoing courage to lead with authenticity when the environment doesn't support that behavior. Charles has posted personal stories about his leadership journey, showing vulnerability and courage in a public forum. He attracted people who believed he would see and hear their own stories. Even then, he was frustrated—why do we make human connection so complicated?

While I cannot answer Charles's question simply, I can describe how leaders can practice inclusion authentically—not just to improve belonging but to fuel innovation and business results. This chapter digs into *why* inclusion is still so elusive, even after decades of well-intended efforts. Understanding that context can empower you to lead differently.

Before understanding what you can do as an individual, as a leader of a team, and as a member of whatever organization you are part of, it is important to absorb a bit of history and the external and internal forces influencing the current business landscape.

Some disclosures: First, I'm writing about what I know best, which is sourced by my research and a few decades of experience supporting leaders in large and small companies across the United States. I'll include global data where I have it. Second, although this book's focus is inclusion and not diversity, this chapter provides essential context to show how the two evolved together—and why separating them now can help us give inclusion the attention it deserves.

From this knowledge, you can make distinctions followed by intentional choices about actions you take. If you are already aware of the historical, external influences that shaped how we got here, feel free to skip ahead. Otherwise, read on.

DIVERSITY AND INCLUSION? IT'S A COMPLICATED RELATIONSHIP

The terms "diversity" and "inclusion" have had a complicated relationship. People have studied diversity for decades. The informative book *Diversity at Work: The Practice of Inclusion* shares articles and essays on the evolution of organizational and societal perspectives and frameworks on diversity and inclusion, the relative newcomer.[1] Dr. Michàlle E. Mor Barak is a distinguished scholar in social work and business management, renowned for her pioneering research on global workforce diversity and inclusion, but even she had to reckon with the attitudes and beliefs of the times. In the preface to the fifth edition of her award-winning book *Managing Diversity: Toward a Globally Inclusive Workplace*, she recounts being told by the publisher of the book's first edition not to use the phrase "inclusive workplace," because no one would know what it meant in that context.[2]

Diversity and inclusion were treated as interchangeable until about fifteen years ago, when researchers began studying inclusion in earnest. More-recent research has focused on how inclusion has evolved to become an enhancement to diversity and the practice of diversity management in organizations.[3] It took decades to get to this point, as the overview of societal, legal, and organizational influences will show. First, another story.

PAST HISTORY INFORMS PRESENT-DAY PRACTICE

Recently I reread *The Pillars of the Earth*, one of a quartet of books that cover hundreds of years of life in England.[4] What a story! The vivid characters and historical events from the Dark Ages to the time of Elizabeth I captivated me. In rereading the story, I noticed that author Ken Follett revealed societal norms that created a huge imbalance of power between groups such as the clergy and others such as women and serfs. One place these imbalances played out was in the Knightsbridge marketplace.

We can use this ancient community event to explain to some degree how we got here, in terms of the enduring and difficult problem of how we treat one another in the workplace. I appreciate that the author used a marketplace as the backdrop and the core for many of the characters and plotlines, which continued from one century to the next. A marketplace is like a modern-day town hall where a cross section of people gather to conduct business, connect with one another, and be part of a community. Here's my adaptation of the marketplace metaphor:

> Picture a vast marketplace at the heart of a thriving city. People from all walks of life flock here. Traders and vendors gather, setting up stalls to showcase their unique goods. Some stalls are grand and expansive, positioned right in the center where foot traffic is constant. Others are modest, tucked into the market's quieter corners. Over time, the marketplace has grown more diverse, with new traders joining from every corner of the world, bringing their spices, textiles, and crafts. But not all traders are treated equally. This is a story of how marketplaces across the country, perhaps even the world, have started, grown, struggled, and evolved to embrace diversity, grappling with inclusion while navigating societal, legal, and cultural forces.

The Early Marketplace: Origins of Inequality

In the early days of the market, not everyone was welcome. The roots of inequality in this marketplace trace back to societal structures that favored a particular group of traders; in the United States, this meant white men. Centuries of history, beginning with the institution of slavery and followed by the exclusion of women and minorities from education, voting, and property ownership, created a foundation upon which the early marketplace was built.

In these early market days, only certain traders had access to the prime spots—the best opportunities. As generations passed, these select stallholders amassed wealth and influence, creating a legacy that continues to impact today's market dynamics. Meanwhile, other traders—especially women, Black individuals, Indigenous peoples, and other minorities—were confined to the fringes, if they were allowed to participate at all. Their voices were unheard, their potential contributions unseen.

By the mid-twentieth century, despite some progress in civil rights, inequality was still deeply embedded in society. In the post–World War II era for instance, the US government introduced the GI Bill to support returning veterans, offering educational and employment opportunities. While the bill's language was neutral, its application was anything but. Black veterans, despite having served their country, were systematically denied access to the benefits that white veterans enjoyed. This led to a significant widening of the wealth gap between white and Black families—a gap that would persist and deepen over the following decades.

The 1960s: A New Era of Market Regulations

It wasn't until the 1960s that the marketplace had a legal reckoning. The Civil Rights Movement brought about a wave of societal change, challenging the deeply entrenched norms of segregation and discrimination. The Civil Rights Act of 1964 was a monumental step. Title VII of this act declared that all individuals, regardless of race, color, religion, sex, or national origin, should have the right to participate in the marketplace without discrimination. This was akin to a decree in the market: "All traders are now welcome to set up stalls."

However, this law only scratched the surface. Within a year, the Equal Employment Opportunity Commission (EEOC) was established to enforce these new rules, taking the market's first steps toward dismantling systemic discrimination. Yet, while the law provided a framework for inclusion, it didn't address the more profound cultural shifts needed to create a marketplace where every trader felt valued and respected. Instead, marketplaces controlled by the same powerful figures continued operating as they always had, selling merchandise they wanted to sell and trying to prevent others from doing the same.

Affirmative action became a crucial tool during this period. President John F. Kennedy first invoked the term in 1961 through Executive Order 10925, calling on organizations to take proactive steps to ensure equal treatment in employment. Four years later, President Lyndon B. Johnson expanded this effort with Executive Order 11246, which forbade discrimination in employment and required federal contractors to take affirmative action to promote equal opportunities for women and minorities.

In practice, affirmative action was a move to level the playing field, much like allocating prime spots in the market to underrepresented traders. It was a way of saying, "We see the imbalance, and we need to take active steps to correct it." Yet, even as more women and minorities began to set up stalls, they still faced numerous obstacles. The rules might have changed on paper, but the attitudes and unspoken norms within the market continued, with discrimination often becoming more covert or nuanced.

1970s–1980s: The Push for Equality—Compliance over Culture

The decades that followed saw companies working to comply with these new legal mandates. Diversity initiatives began to take shape, often focusing on numerical representation: how many women and minorities were hired over a specific time period. Companies were collecting data, tracking the demographics of their workforce, and setting goals to increase diversity, much like market regulators tallying the number of new stalls in the marketplace. But compliance was largely superficial, a matter of checking boxes rather than addressing the deeper issues of inclusion.

Despite these shortcomings, the 1970s and 1980s were vital in laying the groundwork for future efforts. Some companies started to recognize that having a diverse workforce was more than a legal requirement—it could be a strategic advantage. Scholars and business leaders alike began to explore the idea that diversity could lead to improved decision-making, innovation, and performance, though concrete proof was still limited and inclusion was still nowhere to be found in the conversations.

1990s–2000s: The Emergence of Inclusion

By the 1990s, researchers had started to dig deeper into what it meant to create an environment where diversity could thrive. Seminal works during this period laid the foundation for understanding the difference between diversity and inclusion. While diversity was about representation—who is in the market—inclusion was about participation and belonging. The marketplace analogy evolves here: It was no longer enough to merely allow more traders to set up stalls. To foster genuine inclusion, the market needed to become a place where each vendor felt a sense of community, their contributions were valued, and they had access to the same opportunities for growth and success as others.

One of the key academic voices during this time was R. R. Thomas, whose work emphasized the importance of not just diversity but also the cultural changes required to support it.[5] He and other researchers argued that organizations needed to move beyond simple representation and focus on building cultures where every individual felt they belonged. The concept of "inclusion" began to surface more prominently in the workplace lexicon, though it was still often misunderstood, ignored, or conflated with diversity.

M. Mor Barak has spent decades studying global workplaces. Her research went beyond the impact of bringing diverse individuals into an organization, which she considered level one in her model. She names four more levels of spaces where we can think about inclusion: communities, state or national, international, and environmental sustainability.[6] Similarly, the marketplace in Knightsbridge thrived for hundreds of years, at least in part because it became more global. This happened partly out of need—certain commodities could not be obtained locally or required special skills that came from people outside the immediate vicinity—but also because a few key characters understood the symbiotic relationship of the marketplace among not just individuals but also the communities around it in ever-widening circles. Yet those people were not always treated with equity—the people in power still wanted full control over the dealings of those individuals.

Research by Henri Tajfel in 1982 on social identity theory discussed the dynamics of "in-groups" and "out-groups" within organizations and paved the way for scholars to explore the psychological aspects of inclusion in the mid to late 1990s. His theory explained how individuals' sense of belonging to particular groups influenced their perceptions of inclusion and exclusion.[7] As you read this, pause for a moment and think about your own workplace, current or past. How often have you noticed your own or others' behaviors relating to a certain subset of the company population? Perhaps you experienced some cultural benefits because you were part of an in-group, or the opposite was true and you felt the sting of being excluded.

It became evident that creating an inclusive workplace was about more than policies and practices; it required a fundamental shift in how people related to one another.

2000s–2010s: Deeper Understanding of Inclusion

As the new millennium began, the conversation around diversity and inclusion gained momentum. The focus in workplaces shifted from merely counting numbers to understanding experiences. How did employees feel about their places in the organization? Did they feel they could bring their authentic selves to work?

Researchers Ingrid M. Nembhard and Amy C. Edmondson brought the idea of "psychological safety" into the mainstream, further deepening the understanding of inclusion. They found that psychological safety was about creating an environment where individuals felt safe to speak up, take risks, and express their ideas, especially in a team environment, without fear of negative consequences.[8] It became clear that for inclusion to be real, organizations needed to foster this kind of safety, allowing employees to participate fully and bring their unique perspectives to the table.

However, even with this growing awareness, many organizations couldn't seem to move beyond compliance-driven diversity efforts. Maybe you worked at one of these places. They implemented training programs, formed diversity councils, and celebrated cultural holidays, but these actions often remained isolated events rather than integrated components of the organization's culture and strategy. It was as if the marketplace hung banners saying, "Everyone is welcome," while the same barriers persisted at the stalls.

Just as hanging banners is not enough, diversity on its own is insufficient. According to Bernardo M. Ferdman, having diversity without intentional and effective inclusion practices will not enhance organizational performance or employee well-being.[9] Interestingly, research on whether simply having a diverse workforce leads to financial benefits remains limited. A 2017 study assessing the quantitative impact of diversity practices found mixed results. The top fifty companies recognized by DiversityInc for their commitment to diversity did outperform the broader S&P 500 index, but when compared to similar, industry-matched peer companies, they did not demonstrate consistently superior financial performance.[10]

The marketplace continues to grow, but in 2023, the median income for white households in the United States stood at over $106,600, while for Black households, it was just $75,370.[11] This gap in wealth and opportunity mirrored the disparities found in workplaces across the country, highlighting a longstanding issue: The market was open to many but designed and controlled so that only a few could truly thrive.

PERSPECTIVES ON DIVERSITY AND INCLUSION CONTINUE TO EVOLVE

In the early 2010s, studies began to focus on inclusion at in-depth levels.[12] Researchers identified two key elements of inclusive environments for the first time, measuring the degree to which employees felt part of a work group and had their needs met for both uniqueness and belonging. In my own research, I found their description to be the most comprehensive and applicable to the workplace.

When I explain to leaders and teams this two-part definition of inclusion (i.e., "I feel seen and valued for my unique talents and skills, and I also feel like I belong to something bigger than me"), people think about it for a few seconds and nod in agreement. I do not need everyone to think like me, but when I hear people using the term "inclusion," I like to check for understanding and ask, "How do you define it?"

INCLUSION IS STILL AN ENIGMA FOR MANY

This definition of inclusion is purposeful, combining what some people treat as two separate concepts: inclusion and belonging. I often see the words paired together, but not always with clarity about what each one means. Some leaders use them interchangeably; others separate them, as if you can have one without the other. I don't think you can.

Inclusion has always been the quieter part of the diversity/inclusion duo, arriving later to the conversation and still often lumped in. But inclusion as I define it—with belonging built in—offers a more complete picture and is also more workable. It gives leaders a framework to ask, "Do people feel seen here?" and just as importantly, "Do they feel part of something bigger than themselves?" You're welcome to explore definitions that resonate with your workplace, but I encourage you to try this one on. In my experience, it fits.

FROM EVOLVING PERSPECTIVES TO A REVOLVING DOOR

It was only in 2014 that technology companies, including Apple, Facebook, Google, and Microsoft, began to publicly share annual reports on the diversity statistics of their employee populations. According to Sara Harrison in an October 2019 online Wired article, not much had changed since then, despite hundreds of millions of dollars spent, initiatives launched, and hiring efforts increased.[13] Although the percentage of women in some firms has increased, the numbers are still not representative of the overall population, and Black and Latinx employee numbers have barely moved, per a July 2020 Business Insider article.[14] Only Google has reported attrition numbers, and only since 2018; meanwhile, Black and Latinx employees left at higher rates than any other group.

In February 2025, the focus on DEI feels as though it's been slammed into reverse, with a growing list of companies eliminating or drastically cutting back on departments, people, and programs. I won't list those companies here because the speed of the reversal is whiplash fast, and anything I write will be out of date by the time I finish typing this sentence. As of this writing, Google is one of those companies, and I only include it to show the contrast between what it set out to do years ago and where it is now.

Why are women and people of color leaving companies and, in particular, the field of high tech? A US EEOC (2014) report on diversity in high tech noted some interesting themes.[15] First was the enduring prevalence of white men in the field, especially at executive leadership levels, despite their declining representation in the US population overall. Second was the problem of bias in hiring graduates from STEM education programs. For example, underrepresented minorities made up 9 percent of graduates from computer-science programs but only 5 percent of the employee population of the largest tech firms studied. The third theme was factors contributing to attrition, such as unfairness in management practices (e.g., being passed over for promotions, having others take credit for their work, and being given work assignments below their job level) or bias, with women reporting being questioned, ridiculed, or dismissed; having to prove themselves repeatedly; and being ignored or criticized for speaking up.

I was fascinated to learn from my research that companies

in the United States spend billions of dollars and countless hours of people's time on recruiting and hiring a diverse workforce for what appears to be little payoff. One study of about two thousand people who left roles in technology found that the prevailing reason was unfair treatment, including bullying and being denied promotions.[16] It's as if diversity efforts get people through the front door, but when those hires look around and see few or no people like them, especially in leadership roles, they get messages that there is little or no career path for them. Inevitably, they leave, and the cycle begins again, with renewed efforts on getting people through the door and not nearly enough investment of time and effort to ensure the employee population reflects the real-world population, including at various leadership levels.

What sometimes happens is that those who leave start their own marketplace and compete for talent with the same companies that could not keep them. The owners of the marketplace stalls that once thrived risk losing ground in the broader marketplace because they are not keeping up with the evolving skills that future roles require. Potential employees who are learning those new skills may not want to work for companies that don't make an effort to welcome them. Without those workers, companies may lose further ground.

Now that you know more about how we got to where we are today, you might be wondering why we are still here. There is no simple answer to that question, but there are many contributing factors that at least partially answer it.

Let's say you want to make a good effort at improving diversity and inclusion. You are also a business leader who has to produce results. With conviction, you might say, "What gets measured gets managed," and while I would agree with you, in the case of DEI, I have to ask, "What metrics are you using?" and "Managed by whom?"

"Managed by whom?" is usually the first question worth

answering. Diversity metrics were often delegated to the human-resources or equivalent department to be tracked and reported. This is important information and a task that many human-resources professionals would be well qualified to take on.

Now we come to "What metrics are you using?" It is not just the measurement of a quantifiable number. Metrics can be disconnected from any strategic business imperatives. Or they can be disconnected from any genuine cultural integration or understanding of the positive impact of integrating both diversity and inclusion into the flow of daily work processes. Here's an example: Say an organization wants to increase its percentage of women leaders, from the current 27 percent to a future state of 50 percent. To do this, they decide they must increase their ratio by 5 percent a year. But if the company promotes 5 percent more women and 2 percent of the company's women leaders leave in the same year, then it's not sufficient to say, "Hey, we hit our number." The goal of 50 percent women is a metric, and the measure of success needs to be more than just promoting 5 percent more women, because we have to take attrition into account.

The risk that arises is that those metrics are overlooked, undervalued, and managed at likely a very tactical level. Without connection to a long-term strategy, diversity metrics could be diluted and become reactive and short-term, without supportive initiatives to increase the likelihood of achievement.

The handling of diversity metrics that I've described is not always the case. Where it does occur, I invite you to ask, "Who values these metrics?" Do you see senior leaders as active sponsors of the initiatives that get measured? If so, do they seem to understand the ways in which the metrics could contribute to the long-term business strategy? Or are these initiatives part of a long list of activities they are required to support as part of their role? Do these leaders speak about diversity and inclusion every time they discuss longer-term strategy, in the same way they speak about new products or share prices?

If a senior leader or leadership team does not hold themselves accountable for integrating diversity and inclusion directly into their business strategy, it's unlikely they will pass that level of expectation to their direct reports. The senior leaders will have other metrics to hold their teams accountable for—sales, costs, efficiencies, product discovery and launches, patient care, or customer service, to name a few (your company will have its own set of metrics that matter). Many businesses focus on short-term results and quarterly earnings, which can detract from the long-term investments needed to cultivate a truly inclusive and diverse corporate culture.

Even nonprofits have to show results for continued or expanded funding. DEI initiatives often require time to yield tangible business outcomes, and without sustained commitment, these efforts can fall short or fail completely. If there are no role models at the various leadership levels and few or no business leaders are held accountable for the integration of DEI into the business, or if leaders think they are doing enough by inspecting the metrics that others such as human resources reports on, there is no incentive to change. This impasse is tied to the hundreds of years of societal discrimination and racism that predate all of us.

These cultural and subconscious barriers to change could seem justified. What is the benefit of embedding initiatives into the daily rhythm of the organization and designing long-term strategies that enable future outcomes if no one in a position of power thinks they matter? Even with DEI policies in place, deep-seated cultural norms and unconscious biases can undermine inclusion efforts. These barriers to change can prevent diverse talents from fully contributing or advancing in the organization, thus limiting the potential innovation and improved decision-making that diversity can bring.

The needle on these measurements has not moved much in decades. The Kingsbridge market took centuries to grow. We don't have centuries. We face obstacles that are real, complex, and enduring. Our own companies and institutions help perpetuate them, and it's no wonder that the average leader would justifiably ask, "What can I do if the climate around me is not supportive of DEI efforts?"

Here's the hard truth, though: By asking this question, the average leader would be sidestepping another reality. Employees look to their manager for many things: what to pay attention to, what gets rewarded or punished, or what kinds of goals or quotas get measured. In the introduction, I called out leaders as the everyday heroes of inclusion. This chapter affirms this with historical and organizational evidence: While DEI programs come and go, it is the daily choices of managers—how they show up, listen, and lead—that shape whether employees feel they belong.

TODAY

As I write these paragraphs, it is early February 2025. I must pause to reflect on events of the past several weeks that have unfolded in a way I never could have imagined when I began writing in the early summer of 2024.

The administration under the new president of the United States has begun to dismantle DEI programs in federal agencies, lay off people working on any such initiatives, and remove any references to terms such as "diversity," "equity," and "inclusion" on federal agency websites. Several globally recognized companies, including Disney, GE, GM, Google, and Pepsi, have scaled back or deleted references to DEI in annual shareholder reports.

These are just a couple of the headlines that stream across

my news feed. I could go on, but as I, along with thousands or even millions of people in the United States and around the world, process the shock of the speed and scale of these actions, I want to make a point very clearly:

> Now more than ever, people need to know they are respected and valued for who they are. This is a basic human right, and it is not dependent on the degree to which DEI programs are thriving in a company or agency. A colleague who works in the DEI field pointed out that if there is a silver lining to any of this, it is that the notion of DEI as some sort of program has been stripped away. And what is left is the whole point of my book: Employees look to their manager for understanding and examples about the way things work around them and about what matters. They need to feel that they are part of something—call it a community, a purpose, a vision, or whatever you want. Each of us as leaders has an accountability and also an ability to create and sustain an environment where everyone is seen, heard, and recognized for their unique talent and contribution to the company.

Whether you are someone who has been able to rely on a DEI department or partner to help or lead initiatives focusing on diversity, equity, and inclusion, if you are a leader right now in a US company, you have employees who are curious, at best, but likely confused, uncertain, and potentially fearful of what might happen to them, at worst. They are looking to you for answers. I hope that as you continue reading, you will find some.

THE MARKETPLACE OF THE FUTURE

No one knows what the future will bring. Conversely, staying on the same paths we've always trod is almost certain to lead to failure. See the book *The Agility Factor: Building Adaptable Organizations for Superior Performance*, which studies companies that did not adapt and became irrelevant over time.[17] The book also describes companies that demonstrated agility and found success.

Successful adaptation and sustainment of diversity and inclusion means harnessing the power of both without sacrificing either one. The path toward true, scaled, and lasting inclusion is still rocky. As I mentioned earlier, inclusion doesn't happen in workshops alone. This chapter has shown why that matters: We've spent decades implementing programs and checking boxes, but real progress happens when inclusion becomes a daily practice woven into the cultural fabric of work. To foster inclusion practices that allow people to take off their masks requires leaders who model the required behavior, who actively seek out and appreciate diverse perspectives, and who understand that their role is to create an environment where everyone feels safe to be themselves.

Masks can protect our true identity, as evidenced by our superheroes. They can also isolate and separate us from one another. How we got here is a mixture of legal, historical, societal, and organizational norms, customs, dynamics, and practices, many of which were created and maintained by people or groups who want to stay in those positions of power. What they fail to see is that the power of innovation to win in the marketplace requires a broader and deeper pool of capabilities than they can control. For the necessary change, we have to be open to the idea that we ourselves change. More on that in chapter two.

I have stories to tell you about leaders who have done such

things. I have data to suggest the impact of behaving this way. And I offer some ways you can take similar actions. Let's keep exploring what we mean by "inclusionable" so we can get to what is actionable.

CHAPTER ONE SUMMARY

THREE KEY POINTS

1. The journey toward inclusion in the marketplace has deep roots in societal inequities. Early
   efforts focused on compliance, but it wasn't until
   researchers began exploring inclusion in the
   1990s that the conversation expanded to encom-
   pass belonging and participation.

2. Legal changes such as the Civil Rights Act of
   1964 and affirmative action provided the initial
   framework for equality, but they also highlighted
   the complexity of translating legal mandates into
   practical workplace practices.

3. Inclusion is now understood as something that
   leaders can influence regardless of what the
   broader organization is doing. Leaders are role
   models, setting the tone for how inclusion is prac-
   ticed in their part of the marketplace.

THREE REFLECTIVE QUESTIONS

1. How do I define inclusion, and how does this definition align with or differ from how it is understood in my workplace or community?

2. What barriers exist within my team or organization that may be preventing inclusion?

3. How can I, as a leader, model inclusive behaviors and create an environment where every individual feels valued and has a voice?

Feel free to reflect on these questions multiple times and in multiple ways. For example, journaling may not be your thing, but reflection while doing physical exercise might be.

THREE ACTIONS YOU CAN TAKE

1. Engage in conversations. Ask your colleagues how they define inclusion. Listen to their perspectives to understand the diversity of thought within your team or organization.

2. Review what your organization says about diversity and inclusion on its platforms. How has the narrative changed over time, if at all?

3. Educate yourself. Read key articles and books on diversity and inclusion, particularly those that delve into psychological safety, social-identity theory, and the evolving role of inclusive leadership.

CHAPTER TWO

Know Yourself

"You can't lead others until you learn to lead yourself."[1] So says Steve Adubato, PhD, as a chapter title in his book *Lessons in Leadership*. What an apt description of one of the foundational and critical concepts that frame the book you're reading! My research, stories, and examples from interviews will help you deepen your own self-awareness, reflection, and commitment to being an inclusionable leader. No one can do this for you. Your employees need you to be the leader they deserve. You can do this. You are able. This chapter will guide you in leading yourself so you can be a better leader for others.

Knowing yourself is the foundation for all the work you'll do in this space. One of the reasons I wrote this book is to share my own story of self-discovery, not just in terms of understanding inclusion but in how I behave as a leader. This process has been humbling. I always considered myself a lifelong learner, someone who was reflective and adaptive. Perhaps you see yourself that way too. But the truth is, it wasn't until I went through a three-year doctoral program surrounded by a diverse cohort of classmates that I realized how narrow my perspective truly was. I had been relying on my own lived experiences to assess my leadership style and my beliefs around inclusion. That's a limiting lens. In these pages, you will have time to reflect on questions such as "Who are you, first and foremost, as a human being?"

THINK BEYOND YOUR OWN EXPERIENCES

When we look at our own experiences as the primary source of truth, we miss a key point: Our experiences are not universal. They are influenced by who we are—our identities, our upbringing, and our biases. These factors shape how we see the world, how we lead, and how we interact with others. In my case, being a white woman from an upper-middle-class background meant that my personal, societal, and work experiences were vastly different from those of my peers from other racial, ethnic, and socioeconomic backgrounds. What I thought was "inclusive" behavior was really just my interpretation of it, framed by my own context. I had blind spots.

In my doctoral program, we were held accountable for acknowledging and challenging our biases. It was clear that if we were going to truly understand inclusive leadership, we needed to first understand how our identities shaped our perceptions. This process was uncomfortable but necessary. Identity characteristics such as race, gender, and social status heavily influence how we interact with others and how others perceive us as leaders. Without a thorough understanding of this dynamic, it's impossible to create an environment that's truly inclusive.

Before diving into my key research on self-awareness, I

want to share Anderson and Krathwohl's framework, which helped me differentiate types of knowledge.[2] And to truly know yourself, you need to know yourself more deeply than at surface level.

DIVERSITY AND INCLUSION: WHAT'S THE DIFFERENCE?

In my research, many leaders tended to blur the lines between diversity and inclusion. For example, they often listed demographic tracking or diverse-hiring panels alongside role modeling inclusive behaviors or holding career conversations, without recognizing the distinction. This isn't a judgment on them as people, but it does point to a gap in understanding that can limit their effectiveness. That's why this chapter begins with a look at knowledge itself: not just knowing the terms, but understanding how different kinds of knowledge influence how we lead.

Cognitive Knowledge: Understanding the "What"

Understanding the difference starts with cognitive knowledge. At this basic level, leaders need to know what inclusion and diversity mean. In brief, diversity focuses on the representation of different demographic groups, such as gender, race, or ethnicity. Inclusion, on the other hand, is about creating an environment where all individuals feel valued, respected, and able to contribute. While diversity is often a measurable outcome, inclusion is more about the behaviors and practices that enable diverse employees to thrive.

Understanding the distinction between diversity and inclusion allows leaders to choose the right approach for the right situation. Cognitive knowledge provides the necessary foundation for higher-level thinking and action.

Procedural Knowledge: Learning the "How"

Once leaders grasp the cognitive differences between diversity and inclusion, they can move to procedural knowledge—the how. Procedural knowledge focuses on how to implement practices that drive inclusion. For example, it's one thing to understand that fostering inclusion involves active listening, but it's another to know how to cultivate that skill in team meetings. Leaders who have this level of knowledge can integrate inclusive behaviors into their daily leadership practices, such as creating space for different perspectives in decision-making processes or mentoring diverse employees.

Procedural knowledge also involves developing the skills to put inclusive principles into practice. This includes understanding how to create an inclusive environment by promoting open communication, encouraging diverse perspectives, and giving all team members a voice. Leaders who master procedural knowledge are better equipped to turn cognitive understanding into real-world application, fostering workplaces where inclusion is not just a concept but a practice.

Metacognitive Knowledge: Reflecting in Real Time

Real possibility comes when leaders advance to metacognitive knowledge—the ability to reflect on their own thinking and adjust their behaviors accordingly. This is where self-awareness and self-regulation come into play. Leaders who are metacognitively aware can assess their own biases and assumptions about inclusion and diversity, then course correct in real time. For instance, they might recognize that they tend to favor input from certain employees over others, and as a result, they actively work to change that behavior.

In my research, I found that the leaders who engaged in this level of reflection were able to make significant, lasting changes. Half of them made adjustments over time, while others pointed to specific events that prompted them to shift their thinking. By engaging in guided self-monitoring and self-assessment, leaders can strengthen their ability to lead inclusively. This might involve self-reflection exercises during leadership-development programs where leaders log their thoughts and key learnings, or regular feedback sessions with mentors who can provide real-time insights into their behavior. This immediate feedback loop helps leaders adjust their behaviors in the moment and reinforces their commitment to developing inclusive leadership practices.

Metacognitive strategies—monitoring and reflection—help develop inclusive practices. One way to practice is to work on your own biases. For example, logging your thoughts and reactions before, during, and after discussions with others can reveal deeply held beliefs. Noticing them is the first step to taking different action.

FROM KNOWING TO DOING

"Inclusion" and "diversity" are not interchangeable terms, and knowing the difference is the first step to creating an inclusive workplace. Leaders who have a clear cognitive understanding of these concepts can then develop the procedural and meta-cognitive skills needed to bring them to life. The ultimate goal is to create environments where diverse employees feel empowered to contribute, not just be represented in the workforce.

By moving through the stages of cognitive, procedural, and metacognitive knowledge, leaders can shift from simply knowing about inclusion to actively practicing it and reflecting on how they can continuously improve. In doing so, they build the skills necessary to lead inclusively and create a culture where diversity is not just present but truly valued.

ACKNOWLEDGE BLIND SPOTS, BUILD CREDIBILITY

Now that we've explored the layers of knowledge needed to truly know ourselves, here's another question for reflection: "Who are you, as a leader?"

Going a step further than self-awareness means taking a closer look at the beliefs that shape your leadership—beliefs passed down, modeled for you, or formed by experience. Becoming a more inclusive leader requires you to examine those inherited ideas and assumptions, even the ones you've never questioned before. This isn't always comfortable, but it's essential for credibility. Employees can spot when a leader's actions don't match their words. You've likely done so yourself with leaders in your hierarchy. It can be painfully obvious when inclusion is being checked off a list instead of lived out. When you're honest about your learning journey, including what you're still working on, you lay a foundation of trust that makes inclusion real.

In my research, I caught myself falling into assumptions I hadn't named. For example, I realized I often defaulted to "mentor mode" with younger leaders and hesitated to challenge more seasoned ones. These instincts came from unconscious patterns, not conscious decisions. But by becoming aware of those tendencies and actively choosing different responses, I was able to build more respectful and productive relationships across the board.

Owning your blind spots isn't a weakness; it's a strength. It shows your team that you're committed to growing, even when the work is hard. And it signals that inclusion is not just something you expect from others—it's something you're practicing yourself.

SELF-ASSESSMENTS

Think Tools, Not Gospel

Speaking of biases, I confess I have a bias about self-assessments in general, which is that they can take on an outsize role in your journey of self-awareness. In the world of personal development and leadership, self-assessments can be like religious or political affiliations of the professional sphere. People discover a framework—such as DiSC, Myers-Briggs Type Indicator (MBTI), Enneagram, CliftonStrengths (formerly StrengthsFinder), Hogan Personality Inventory (HPI), the Big Five Personality Test (also known as the five-factor model), or countless others out there—and become evangelists for it, convinced it's the one true key to understanding themselves and others. For a more detailed description of these frameworks, see the resources section.

This passion is not without merit; these tools can be transformative. I am certified in and/or have used many of them. But here's the rub: No single assessment is perfect, and none of them hold the monopoly on self-awareness. To truly benefit from self-assessments, I recommend approaching them with a certain mindset. Let's unpack how to make the most of these tools without falling into the trap of blind allegiance.

Fill Your "Toolbox"

When I bought my first home, I assumed that a hammer, a screwdriver, some pliers, and a wrench would be enough. To my surprise, I realized different screws required different tools—just like leadership assessments. I could do many things with the tools, or assessments, I started out with, but eventually I needed other tools. Likewise, each self-assessment offers unique insights:

- DiSC excels at helping teams understand behavioral styles in the workplace.
- The Herrmann Brain Dominance Instrument (HBDI) explores how individuals think and process information.
- The Enneagram delves deep into motivations and fears that drive behavior.

If we think of each self-assessment as being a unique tool in the toolbox, we can use them together instead of limiting ourselves to only one type. Taken together in a fit-for-purpose way, various assessments will provide a fuller picture of who you are.

A Map Is Not the Real Terrain

Here's another tool metaphor, using an app this time. When I ride my road bike, I use a GPS app to guide me on my route. It can show me turns, elevation, and distance, but it can't tell me if a rainstorm this morning caused a road to flood, or whether construction that was supposed to be finished last week is actually completed, or that the annual music festival in my neighborhood might require a completely different route. A self-assessment is like a map—it gives you a high-level view of your personality, preferences, and tendencies. But maps, no matter how detailed, are abstractions of the real world. They help you navigate but don't capture the full complexity of the terrain. For example, MBTI might report preferences that suggest you identify as an INFP (introverted, intuitive, feeling, perceiving), emphasizing introversion and feeling, but it won't tell you how you've adapted those traits in response to life's challenges. Or CliftonStrengths might highlight your talent for strategic thinking, but it won't pinpoint when or how that strength, if overused, could become a weakness.

All good tools have a specific purpose, but to use a tool differently than it was intended or to think that your favorite tool is the only tool you ever need can diminish possibilities for growth or result in missing out on other possibilities or complications.

I suggest that we rely on these tools for direction, but remember they are simplifications, not the whole truth.

Beware of the Confirmation Bias Trap

Once people identify with a certain assessment, they often begin to see everything through its lens. For example, as someone with a preference in MBTI for gathering data via abstract, conceptual, and original thinking, I tend to see myself as *not* attending to details in realistic or practical terms. I therefore shy away from work that requires a lot of details. That impacts choices I make about jobs I have applied for or stayed away from.

While these insights can be empowering, overidentifying can lead to rigidity. You are a dynamic, evolving individual. Challenge yourself to seek insights from assessments that may initially feel "wrong" or counter to your self-perception. Growth often lies in the areas that assessments don't capture neatly.

Focus on Application, Not Labels

The real power of self-assessments lies in what you do with the information. Understanding that you're a "visionary" according to CliftonStrengths or an "extravert" in MBTI doesn't mean much unless you apply it. Ask yourself:

- How does this insight help me improve my relationships?

- In what ways will I use this knowledge to lead more effectively?
- Which blind spots do I now see that I can address?

Information and knowledge about assessments create a common language among those who use them. Sadly, I have seen that knowledge used to label others. Using assessment language to label people can create a feeling of exclusion. This has happened to me, and you might have experienced something similar: "Oh, you are a 7; that explains it." People in the group who know the Enneagram nod in agreement, and I feel part of an out-group because I am not trained in that tool and have no idea what they are talking about.

I am not criticizing the Enneagram; it is a great tool for self-assessment. And while I am certified in the use of MBTI, I have had to correct people around me who have made blanket statements like "Well, the introverts must not have anything to say, or else they would speak up" or "Quiet people don't make good bosses because you never know what is on their minds." All assessments are starting points, not endpoints. Their value comes from turning knowledge into action, not making statements of opinion as if they were facts.

Stay Curious and Open

Just as no one religion or political system has all the answers, no self-assessment provides a complete understanding of human behavior. Staying curious means continuously exploring new frameworks, even if you already have a favorite. No assessment serves all purposes, and every assessment has a contribution to make when you are ready. If we can remain open to the possibilities, we can better serve ourselves and our teams with humility, recognizing that growth is ongoing and no single tool will ever "solve" the puzzle of who you are.

You are not your MBTI (or Enneagram, or DiSC, or any other assessment) type. Self-assessments are powerful allies on your journey of self-awareness and leadership, but they are not definitive verdicts on your character or destiny. Embrace their strengths, acknowledge their limitations, and use them as part of a larger effort to understand yourself and others. By doing so, you'll become an even more well-rounded, self-aware, and inclusionable leader. In the end, the best assessment is not the one that defines you perfectly—it's the one that sparks the greatest growth and awareness.

AWARENESS LEADS TO ACTION

In my research, I asked leaders to describe a time when they became aware of their own biases or assumptions and how that awareness influenced their actions. Almost universally, leaders described self-awareness as a precursor to meaningful change. Simply put, you can't change what you don't acknowledge.

One leader shared how this process began with the realization that, as a senior leader, they often felt the need to jump in and fix problems. But over time, they learned that leading inclusively meant slowing down, listening more, and empowering others to find solutions themselves. "It's not about fixing everything," they said. "It's about asking, 'What can I bring to this situation that will help others feel heard and included?'"

Listening as a Strategy for Inclusion

Another leader described the discipline of listening as a daily practice. "I really try to listen better every day. It's like homework," they said. "I have to remind myself to focus on what others are saying before jumping to conclusions." That leader was authentic and concise in describing a universal problem for leaders. Aren't we paid to take action and achieve results? Weren't we hired or promoted because we have a proven track record of knowing what to do? That may be true, but it puts all the responsibility for the solution on me as the leader, and sooner or later I will make a mistake or miss an opportunity.

Listening, deep listening, is incredibly difficult to do. For me, it means hushing the chatter in my mind and resisting the urge to quickly flick through my mental file folders labeled "Similar Problems" or "Been There, Done That" to find the right answer, often while the other person is still talking! We all want to be thought of as capable, smart, and accomplished, but if we look at every problem only in terms of what we already know, we will fail deeply when new problems emerge (and they will) or new conditions for success are needed. Leaders who don't listen—who constantly dominate conversations or interrupt—miss the chance to hear diverse perspectives.

Listening goes beyond just hearing words; it's about being fully present and open to other perspectives. As leaders, we can often dominate the room, consciously or unconsciously shutting down voices that differ from our own. True inclusion happens when we listen to understand, not just to respond. I gathered some great insights during my interviews. One leader described how they had developed the practice of "getting quiet" during meetings to allow space for others to speak. They would explicitly tell their team, "I'm going to step back and listen now," signaling that they were creating room for other voices. This level of self-awareness not only fosters inclusion but also sets a powerful example for others on the team.

Leaders must recognize that the tendency to jump in with solutions can stifle the very creativity and innovation that diversity brings to the table. By pausing, listening, and being open to diverse ideas, leaders can foster a more inclusive and dynamic environment.

The Role of Feedback in Leadership Growth

Accepting feedback—especially when it contradicts self-perception—is challenging. Yet many leaders I spoke with had their most profound moments of self-awareness after receiving difficult feedback. One leader shared how they were shocked by the results of their first 360-degree review, a way of collecting feedback about someone from people who play different roles in their work. Feedback in a 360-degree review typically comes from the individual, their manager, peers, direct reports, customers, and others who interact with the individual. This leader explained, "I thought I was being intentionally inclusive, but the feedback said otherwise. I was frustrated. How could my perception be so different from what others were experiencing?"

This disconnect between intent and impact is common. As leaders, we often believe that our actions align with our values. But without regular, honest feedback, we may not realize how others perceive us. Inclusive leadership requires being open to feedback—especially when it's uncomfortable. It's through this feedback that we can identify our blind spots and begin to make meaningful changes.

Empathy: The Heart of Inclusive Leadership

A core characteristic at the heart of inclusive leadership is empathy—the ability to understand and share the feelings of others. But empathy doesn't happen in a vacuum. It requires self-awareness. Leaders who haven't taken the time to reflect on their own biases and assumptions will struggle to empathize with those who have different experiences and perspectives.

Empathy is about more than just understanding someone else's feelings; it's about taking action to support them. In an inclusive work environment, empathy means recognizing the unique challenges faced by underrepresented groups and making adjustments to ensure that everyone feels valued and included. This could mean providing mentorship opportunities, creating flexible work policies, or simply being more attuned to the needs of individuals on your team.

You're Setting the Tone (Whether You Mean To or Not)

One thing that surprised me in my research was how many leaders wrestled with the idea that others were watching them for cues on how to act. Some fully embraced it. One leader told me she regularly brought together colleagues who normally wouldn't interact, knowing that these seemingly small moments created ripples. Another said, "The best kind of influence comes from people who are real. If you hide your flaws, no one trusts you."

But not everyone felt at ease with the spotlight. A few cringed at the idea of being called a role model. One very senior leader admitted, "I get embarrassed just talking about it." That discomfort makes sense. Most of us weren't raised to think of ourselves as examples. And in a culture that often confuses visibility with ego, claiming influence can feel arrogant. But here's the thing: You're already influencing others, whether you mean to or not. People are paying attention. They notice how you treat others, what you prioritize, how you respond to mistakes. You're already shaping the culture around you—consciously or not.

What struck me even more was the organizational silence around this topic. When I reviewed leadership documents from one company, I found no clear expectations for what visible leadership looked like when it came to inclusion. No definitions. No stories. No guideposts. It left many leaders guessing. As I reflected on that, I realized I'd made an assumption in my interviews: I asked people about being role models without ever asking what that meant to them. I had my own mental picture, but I never paused to say, "What does it mean to you?" That's part of my learning journey too.

To be accountable means to be inclusionable. Leadership sets the tone for the entire organization. If you want to create an inclusive environment, you can begin by holding yourself accountable for the environment you're fostering. I know from speaking with dozens of leaders that it's tempting to say that the culture above or beyond your area of control is in dire need of change. It's those leaders that never seem to show up at the DEI workshops or have proof they are doing any of the things they ask us to do in their quarterly all-hands meetings. Here's a truth to try on, though: No matter what is happening in the environment around you, you have agency (and therefore accountability) in your own circle of influence. You have agency; why not put it to use in a way that influences for good?

To be clear, leaders universally, and for as long as I've been in companies, deal with this issue. The "circle of influence" refers to the range of things you can directly control or significantly impact, while a "circle of concern" encompasses all the things you are worried about, even if you have little to no control over them. The circle of influence is the subset of concerns that one can actively manage, while the circle of concern is the broader set of worries that may not be directly actionable. These concepts were brilliantly described by Stephen R. Covey in his book *The 7 Habits of Highly Effective People*.[3]

If it's difficult to imagine how two intersecting circles apply to your regular workday, here is an alternative. Think of one hour of time. The seconds and minutes tick by regardless of what you are doing or thinking. Notice how much of that hour you spend thinking about things you cannot control, such as sales budgets assigned to your department, or the person who cut you off while changing lanes on the way to work, or the rumor you heard about another round of layoffs. Before you know it, most of that hour is gone, and you feel more anxious, drained, or uncertain about what to do next. Each minute of worry expands your circle of concern, until it becomes a huge burden. How satisfying is that?

I can't give you that hour back, but I can help you with the next hour. You can choose to think about those things you *can* influence. You can focus on the meetings you host or bringing your curiosity and collaboration to a new group. Instead of waiting for a team member to take action and being frustrated when they don't, you can go to them and suggest you work together for half an hour on that task. When you start to expand your circle of influence, your circle of concern will shrink. Notice how good it feels to have a larger circle of influence! You have a greater opportunity then to notice how it feels to achieve a result, even a modest one. You've got this.

The good news is that with all this accountability, you can really have an impact. It means being intentional about the way you lead, the policies you implement, and the behaviors you model. Inclusion doesn't happen by accident—it's the result of deliberate effort. It requires more than just good intentions. It demands action, reflection, and a willingness to grow. By holding yourself accountable, you create a culture where inclusion isn't just an ideal but a reality.

One practical way to build accountability is by integrating self-reflection and feedback into your leadership routine. Set aside time to reflect on your own behaviors and how they align with your goals for inclusion. Seek out feedback from your team—especially from those whose perspectives differ from your own. And most importantly, be willing to make changes based on that feedback.

CHAPTER TWO SUMMARY

THREE KEY POINTS

1. Becoming an inclusive leader doesn't happen
    overnight. It's a journey that requires continuous
    reflection, learning, and growth. And we never
    arrive at a particular destination.

2. Understand and celebrate your increasing aware-
    ness of your biases and assumptions. Limitless
    opportunities for growth and fulfillment come
    from revealing yourself to yourself.

3. Accountability leads to "inclusionability." Accept
    that you have influence over your team and that
    people look to you for examples, for direction,
    for support, or for what matters. From that place
    of awareness, you can begin to innovate and
    experiment.

THREE REFLECTIVE QUESTIONS

1. What are my core values?

2. What do I assume or believe about leadership,
    and where or how did I learn that?

3. Who am I a role model for today? How am I
    showing up for them?

THREE ACTIONS YOU CAN TAKE

1. To further develop your self-awareness, use journaling, get perspective from a trusted colleague, or engage in feedback exercises such as 360-degree reviews.

2. Listen more, talk less. Practice the discipline of listening—really listening—to your team. Create space for diverse voices and be open to ideas that challenge your own. Tell others that you are doing this, and invite them to support you by pointing out when or if you might slip into old patterns or show a bias for action too soon.

3. Embrace empathy. Put yourself in others' shoes, and take action to support them. Whether it's through mentorship, advocacy, or simply being more attentive to the needs of individuals, empathy is key to fostering inclusion.

CHAPTER THREE

Know Your Team

"Not finance. Not strategy. Not technology. It is teamwork that remains the ultimate competitive advantage, both because it is so powerful and so rare."

This is a quote from Patrick Lencioni from *The Five Dysfunctions of a Team: A Leadership Fable.*[1] What I find so powerful about this quote is that after thirty years of working with leaders and teams, I know it is true. I have shared it in classes I teach and during leadership team off-site meetings, and I get the same response. People nod their heads. They chuckle in a knowing way. They get it.

Most people have been part of a team at some point—whether in work, sports, school, or community life. And most people have experienced both great teams and dysfunctional ones. Why is teamwork so hard? Lencioni boils it down to two main reasons. Teamwork is difficult to measure. It also requires unrelenting commitment. There are likely other reasons, but these two capture the essence of what he is saying very well.

TEAMWORK IS DIFFICULT TO MEASURE

To me, measuring teamwork is like trying to measure the degree of impact the sun has on growing crops. We know it makes a difference, but how much of a difference? How can we tell the degree to which teamwork contributed to a team achieving its objectives? There are so many variables involved, including the degree of organizational support for teams, the skill sets of each individual, the number of priorities senior leaders set, and the quality of the product the company sells. No wonder senior leaders measure everything and anything other than teamwork.

TEAMWORK REQUIRES UNRELENTING COMMITMENT

Lencioni points out that teamwork cannot be treated like a commodity that is bought and sold on the open market. In his follow-up book *Overcoming the Five Dysfunctions of a Team: A Field Guide for Leaders, Managers, and Facilitators*, he states that teamwork requires "levels of courage and discipline—an emotional energy—that even the most driven executives don't always possess."[2] I find this statement to also be true.

If great teamwork takes laser focus and relentless commitment, it's no wonder a leader might flinch. Maybe you have felt this yourself. It is easier to bypass the work to know ourselves and how we operate and instead go straight to the "important" work of setting goals and metrics. Those activities feel tangible and real. The other stuff—the business of building a team? They might be called soft skills, but in reality, those skills can be incredibly hard to develop, especially if we never spend time on them.

You might be feeling a bit deflated by now. If you agree with these declarations, what is there for you to do? Plenty, as it turns out. If you can tune out the politics, the pressure, and the conflicting priorities that come at you and your team for even short periods of time, you can accomplish a lot together by attending to some basic principles. First, grab a cup of tea or coffee or take a quick five-minute walk around your block, and take a few deep breaths. Some pretty exciting stuff is coming up.

Right, then, here you are. You are leading a team of perhaps one or two, or ten or twelve people. Maybe it is a much bigger team. Or perhaps you now lead an organization made up of several teams, each one separate, but all of them—sales, marketing, engineering, finance, human resources, product development, manufacturing, and so on—need to interact with one another as part of the organization's work processes. I'll focus on knowing the larger system you're part of in the next chapter. In the rest of this chapter, to keep things simple, I'll use your team of direct reports.

Regardless of the size of the team, you are in charge. Whether you are new to the role or have been in it for a while, pause for a moment to consider what you know about the group. A few questions to get you started: Who are the individuals, and what are their separate needs and strengths? What goals, what results, what strengths, and what areas of opportunity does this team have? You want to do a good job of leading them, and you want to be inclusive.

As you think about these questions, how do you proceed? I find that one way to work on an issue or problem is by applying a framework. You'll see several of them in this book. And I see an intersection point between a sixty-year-old model and inclusionable practices.

BRUCE TUCKMAN'S STAGES OF TEAM DEVELOPMENT

About sixty years ago, Bruce Tuckman developed a model of

the stages of team development as a practical way to make sense of how people working together in groups or teams grow and develop over time. His easy-to-understand terms for the phases gave people a common language to discuss their own team dynamics. Tuckman's model—forming, storming, norming, performing, and adjourning—remains relevant, even as teams shift stages due to reorganizations or new dynamics. If you want to look into the Tuckman model in more detail, you can find books about applying it through online resources like Amazon. Whether or not you are already familiar with the model, you might find it helpful. In this chapter, I'll connect each stage of team development with actions you can take as a leader to enhance your team members' feelings of inclusion. Models are always easier to understand with a visual:[3]

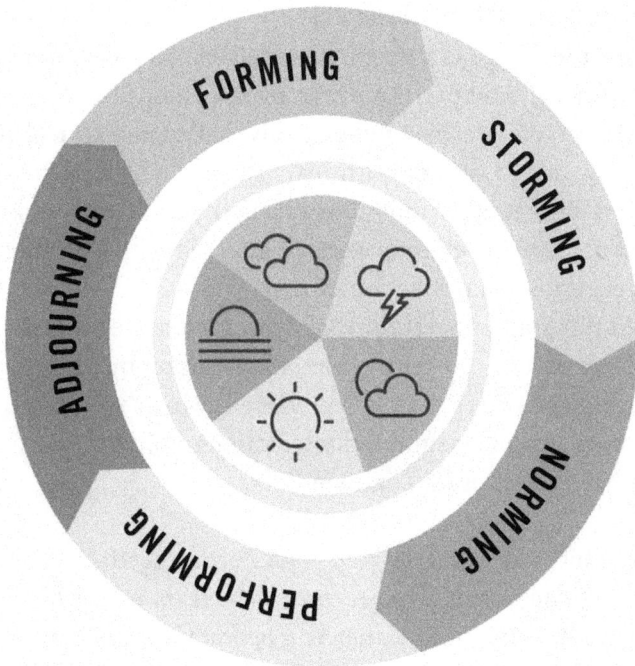

Figure 1. Bruce Tuckman's Stages of Team Development diagram by DovileMi.

Business leaders often grapple with fostering inclusive environments while simultaneously guiding teams through natural stages of development. Bruce Tuckman's model provides a valuable framework for understanding group dynamics. When paired with intentional inclusionary practices, leaders can enhance employee engagement, team cohesion, and productivity.

I'll share a short description of the kinds of team behavior you might experience in each stage, based on my own observations as a team member, team leader, and team coach for several decades. Then I'll share some practices I've used and that I know work well, again based on experience, trial and error, and even failure.

The Forming Stage

Build Trust and Welcome Diversity

The forming stage is sometimes called the honeymoon phase. Regardless of whether the whole team is new to one another or one person is a new joiner, individuals need to feel their way. One team I worked with years ago had what one member called a "veneer of harmony," where on the surface all was well, but at a deeper level, they were all guarded with one another, not yet certain who they could trust.

At this stage, uncertainty is high—for both team members and leaders. You can set the tone for inclusion by fostering an environment where people feel valued, which requires time, commitment, and structured interactions.

A few practices I recommend:

- Introduce and develop team norms together.
  Team norms are agreements the team makes together about how they will operate. Some examples include: We will meet weekly for one hour; we will respect personal time and not text or chat

each other between 7 p.m. and 7 a.m.; or we will each name a backup if we are going to be out of office for more than two days.

• Begin by sharing a few norms you value and asking team members to collaboratively build on that list. One of my favorite team norms is "take space and make space," which asks the talkative team members to consciously manage their tendency to constantly share ideas and suggestions, allowing quieter team members to add their comments on a more regular cadence. Knowing that either behavior might feel uncomfortable, you as the leader can take the opportunity to connect this norm with respect for diverse perspectives. People want to know they are valued for their skills and expertise; when they do, they will more likely feel appreciated and that they belong.[4]

• Facilitate icebreaker activities that allow members to share aspects of their backgrounds, skills, and experiences. This not only builds trust but also signals that each person's identity and story contribute meaningfully to the team.

• Support the team's collective development as well as individual growth and development. Few things show how much you care as does investing time, effort, and even money to support someone's career path and their personal and professional growth. I want to underscore the need to do this proactively, beyond being available if they want to talk or having a career conversation once a year as part of a performance-evaluation process. Knowing what each person aspires to is a start, and allyship, networking, and approving training where it makes sense will go a long way.

◆   Model openness and curiosity, demonstrating an eagerness to learn from all team members.

In this phase, leaders should emphasize behaviors such as empathy, active listening, and creating psychological safety—a foundation for inclusive behavior that, according to Amy Edmondson, is crucial for a team's long-term success.[5] In addition, one of the most effective actions you can take to get to know your team members—not just their skills and qualifications but also their personalities, working styles, and motivations—is through assessments. In the previous chapter on knowing yourself, I advocated for a toolbox approach, where no one assessment serves all purposes, but every well-designed assessment can be a tool or a map for self-discovery. The same can be said for a team's use of assessments. Used thoughtfully, assessments can accelerate and enhance team members' understanding and embracing of one another's differences.

The Power of Assessments in the Forming Stage

When a team first comes together, its members often operate from assumptions about one another. Without tools to surface and explore differences, these assumptions can lead to misunderstandings, misalignment, and missed opportunities. Introducing an assessment during the forming stage helps to create a shared language around individual preferences, strengths, and styles, and provides leaders and teams with a structured way to understand and appreciate differences.

For leaders, the insights gleaned from these assessments can be eye-opening. Has this happened yet for you? Assessments provide a road map for understanding communication preferences, decision-making styles, and other elements of working together—insights that might otherwise take months to discover. Here's a story from my own experience:

Many, many years ago, I went through MBTI certification

training along with my peers and my manager. We all worked in a human-resources department together, and we wanted to use what we learned to help the teams we supported work more effectively together. What I didn't imagine at the time was that I would learn a lifelong lesson about my own ways of working with others.

Almost from the day I started working in the company, I wondered if my manager actually liked me. My office was about sixty feet down the hall from my manager's, and being a collaborative kind of person, I would often walk down the hall to chat. I would politely knock on the doorframe (the door was open, suggesting my manager was available) and say, "I just want to run something by you." I often saw a look (was it panic, discomfort, or uncertainty?) cross my manager's face so fast I wasn't sure if I imagined it.

"Sure, come in" was the usual reply. I would sit down and start to brainstorm ideas about how to handle something. I got irritated when I realized my manager was going into problem-solving mode. "No, I don't want to solve the problem right now; I just want to talk about it" was my frequent thought. When I would leave my manager's office, I usually sensed that we were both dissatisfied with the outcome. This went on for months.

My life changed dramatically after learning about MBTI. Once I saw that people tend to have preferences about the ways we get energy, take in information, make decisions about that information, and orient ourselves to the world and that these different preferences are not good or bad, I let go of the idea that my manager was being difficult or didn't like me. I realized my manager and I simply had very different preferences. My manager preferred some advance notice about the topic I wanted to discuss, even if it was a short verbal description or a few bullet points in an email. I tend to think while I talk and talk while I think. We were experiencing the introverted/extraverted dynamic. My manager wanted more details (sensing preference) while I was still exploring patterns, possibilities, and abstract thoughts (intuition), and even though I was happy to stay open to new information and ideas before deciding (perceiving), my manager thought that I needed to, wanted to, or should make a decision, have closure, and move on. Otherwise, why had I come to talk about the topic?

Inclusion Through Shared Exploration

The act of completing an assessment together as a team goes beyond the individual insights it provides. It becomes a shared experience that fosters openness and trust. When team members discuss their results in a facilitated session, they begin to see differences not as obstacles but as assets. In my case, I realized how much I need people with a preference for data-driven decision-making that complements my love of big-picture thinking.

If you can be a leader who models curiosity and respect during this process, you can set the tone for an inclusive culture. In addition, assessments help surface unconscious biases or assumptions that might otherwise go unaddressed. I talked about this in the previous chapter, and in the case of team dynamics, a team member who initially seems aloof may simply have an introverted preference, while someone who dominates early discussions might have a high level of assertiveness. Naming and framing these traits as necessary differences for the sake of the team's effectiveness creates space for all voices to be heard.

Practical Tips When Using Assessments in the Forming Stage

To maximize the impact of assessments, I recommend that you:

- Select the right tool for the team's needs. Choose an assessment that aligns with the team's goals and context. For new teams, tools that focus on communication and collaboration styles are especially useful. You might need help with this, and I provide some references in the resources section.

- Facilitate a thoughtful debrief. A debrief session is essential for translating assessment results into actionable insights. Use this time to draw connections between individual styles and team dynamics. I highly recommend you get help from an expert to do this, for two reasons. First, as a leader, you want to participate in discussions about team results, and you can't do that if you are facilitating. Second, some assessments require certification to use, but at the very least, you want someone who is experienced with the content and the context of how to interpret the results.
- Revisit assessments regularly. Teams evolve, and so do their needs. Periodic reassessments can reveal shifts in dynamics and keep the team aligned. This is especially true in the rest of the stages of team development. Whether a team is storming, norming, performing, or adjourning, knowing about team members' individual preferences will help for a smoother (not completely flawless) transition. In the resources section, you'll find more assessments that offer diagnostics and actions for teams in every stage of development.
- Leverage insights to tailor your leadership. Understanding team assessments enables leaders to adjust their approach—whether by delegating tasks according to strengths, mediating conflicts with empathy, or fostering inclusion through tailored communication.

By incorporating assessments into the forming stage and making them a collaborative experience, leaders lay the groundwork for a more inclusive, cohesive, and high-performing team. These tools aren't just about diagnosing differences—they're about celebrating and leveraging them for the collective good.

I want to return to something I have already mentioned. A very important reason to take time and intention at the forming stage is that when people are feeling at their most guarded and vulnerable, you can do a lot to build trust.

Vulnerability, Authenticity, and the Role of Trust in Team Success

Team assessments ask individuals to open a window into their inner world—their preferences, strengths, and, at times, limitations. This process inherently requires a degree of vulnerability. To answer questions about how we communicate, make decisions, or approach conflict, team members must reveal truths about themselves that might not align with how they want to be perceived. Leaders who recognize and honor this vulnerability can create an environment where authenticity thrives, laying the foundation for trust.

Trust, as researchers have long established, is a critical ingredient for high-performing teams. It comes in two forms: cognitive trust and affective trust. Cognitive trust is task based; affective trust is built on emotional connection and shared vulnerability. I have to believe that if I'm going to reveal myself to you, you will reciprocate in kind with me.

While cognitive trust is essential for ensuring the team believes in one another's abilities, affective trust is the glue that holds a team together during challenges, fostering collaboration, innovation, and resilience.

Team assessments provide a powerful opportunity to build both forms of trust. When team members share their results and engage in discussions about their styles and strengths, cognitive trust grows—they see evidence of each person's contributions. Simultaneously, affective trust emerges as individuals share personal stories, admit areas for growth, and express their needs in a space that promotes mutual respect. For this to happen, leaders must model vulnerability, setting the tone by sharing their own results and embracing the insights without defensiveness.

Psychological Safety

At the heart of a successful, inclusive team is psychological safety—the shared belief that the team is a safe space for interpersonal risk-taking. Research by Amy Edmondson highlights that in psychologically safe teams, members feel empowered to voice ideas, ask questions, and admit mistakes without fear of judgment or reprisal.[6] Psychological safety isn't one size fits all. When the topic comes up, I usually ask, "Whose definition of safety are we using?" And almost always, the other person pauses, purses their lips, and goes "hmmmm."

For some, safety might mean having the freedom to challenge the status quo, while for others, it might mean the assurance that they won't be singled out or excluded for their differences. Team assessments, when done with care, allow leaders to uncover these varying definitions and address them explicitly. By discussing what safety means to each team member, leaders can foster a culture that accounts for diverse perspectives and experiences.

If you can facilitate these conversations and integrate assessment insights into team practices (and remember that I think you can), you will take meaningful steps toward building both trust and inclusion. Demonstrate that vulnerability is not a weakness but a pathway to connection, authenticity, and, ultimately, success and your team may well start modeling your behavior. At the very least, you can create a team environment where members feel both competent and cared for—where trust is not just built but actively nurtured over time.

The Storming Stage

Navigate Conflict and Embrace Differences

The storming stage is marked by competition, disagreements, and the testing of boundaries as team members assert their ideas. While conflict can be constructive, unaddressed tensions can erode trust and engagement.

Key inclusionary practices in storming:

* Normalize constructive conflict by establishing guidelines that encourage differing viewpoints while maintaining respect. Leaders can remind team members that diverse ideas often lead to better problem-solving and innovation.
* Act as mediator and advocate, ensuring that all voices are heard—especially those who may be more reserved. Inclusive leaders actively encourage participation by balancing the power dynamics within the team.[7]
* Reframe challenges by focusing on shared goals. Highlighting common objectives helps mitigate the polarization that can arise from differing opinions.

During the storming phase, leaders should maintain a keen awareness of their team's emotional climate and intervene appropriately to sustain an inclusive, respectful dialogue.

The Norming Stage

Reinforce Belonging and Shared Values

As the team enters the norming stage, members begin to find their roles, establish mutual trust, and align with shared standards and values. Leaders play a critical role in reinforcing newly established norms to deepen a sense of belonging.

Key inclusionary practices in norming:

• Celebrate milestones and achievements to foster collective pride and emphasize the value each member brings. This could be as simple as recognizing contributions during meetings or highlighting individual skills in team communications.

• Create inclusive rituals, such as weekly feedback sessions or open forums where members can voice opinions without fear.

• My research found that leaders who engage others in critical decisions tend to foster the most inclusive climates. To do so required seeking input and perspective from everyone present.[8] Notice the word "critical" in this practice. Not every decision needs full consensus; efficiency matters. And it is true that consulting everyone present takes time and is often overlooked for the sake of fast decision-making. Yet the payoff can be twofold: First, engagement by people who felt included in important decisions increased, and second, the likelihood of making better decisions also increased because of the broader range of expertise and knowledge being tapped.

• The beauty of this action is that you can begin it at any time. If you did not have an opportunity to create a team norm about decision-making in the forming stage, you can certainly do it in either the storming stage (where having a more robust decision-making process can help ease the storming tendencies) or as part of the norming stage.

• Develop shared language that includes terms and references reflective of the team's collective identity and diverse backgrounds. Inclusive leaders are mindful of using culturally sensitive language that reinforces unity.

The norming phase offers leaders an opportunity to solidify inclusive practices that will anchor the team as it progresses into high performance.

The Performing Stage

Enhance Contributions and Innovation

In the performing stage, the team reaches optimal functionality, marked by high morale, efficient processes, and collaborative synergy. This phase demands sustained inclusion to keep team members engaged and motivated.

Key inclusionary practices in performing:

- Encourage continuous learning by inviting team members to share new insights and experiences. You do not need special training to host peer-learning opportunities or discussion groups that allow team members to showcase their expertise.
- Solicit input and feedback on decision-making to ensure diverse perspectives are integrated into strategic planning. Research by McKinsey & Company showed that organizations in the top quartile for ethnic and cultural diversity are 36 percent more likely to outperform their peers.[9]
- Empower team autonomy while maintaining a supportive presence. Leaders should trust team members to execute their roles effectively while remaining available for guidance.

Inclusion in the performing stage enhances commitment and helps maintain peak performance over time.

The Adjourning Stage

Honor Contributions and Facilitate Transitions

The adjourning stage involves the disbanding of the team, whether after the completion of a project or when roles are reassigned. It is the one stage that often gets ignored as new projects come along and team members scatter without formal closure of what they worked on together. Yet this stage can be emotionally complex, and leaders must prioritize inclusivity to ensure that all members feel acknowledged and respected.

Key inclusionary practices in adjourning:

- Conduct formal reflections and debrief sessions to allow team members to share their experiences and lessons learned. These discussions should recognize each individual's impact on the team's journey.
- Celebrate the conclusion with inclusive rituals, such as group celebrations, awards, or individual notes of appreciation. As a team leader, you can have the pleasure of honoring the unique contributions of each member. In doing so, keep in mind that people also have different preferences about acknowledgment. I have a colleague who would rather have a root canal at the dentist than be recognized in public for her excellent work. Make the celebration and recognition appropriate to what the person or people being honored would like.
- Provide transitional support, such as connecting team members with future opportunities within the organization. Leaders can maintain an inclusive culture by advocating for continued growth and development.

The adjourning stage represents an important moment for leaders to strengthen a culture of appreciation and set the stage for future inclusive team practices.

Applying inclusionary practices across all five stages of Tuckman's model enables leaders to create a team environment where members feel seen, valued, and integral to the group's success. By fostering trust in the forming stage, navigating conflict inclusively in storming, reinforcing belonging during norming, empowering contribution in performing, and honoring the team during adjourning, leaders can guide their teams toward high performance and sustained engagement.

These practices are not just beneficial; they are essential for long-term business success in today's diverse workplace. I am mindful of another quote by Patrick Lencioni: "Teams exist to produce results."[10] For all the effort that goes into building and guiding a team through stages of development, there will always be expectations that the team exists to produce a certain result over a specific period of time. This suggests performance goals.

I was curious what leaders needed to do to incorporate inclusionary practices into their performance goals. One question I posed in interviews was in what ways did leaders monitor their own biases when bringing inclusionary practices into performance goals. I got some valuable insights from those discussions. All but one of the interviewees showed awareness that leaders may need to act differently when interacting with their teams. In certain cases, leaders I spoke with gave many examples demonstrating that they reflected on, adjusted, and monitored their skills or behavior as part of improving their inclusionary practices. One leader, for instance, realized she needed to be quiet and let people share insights before she made any comments. Her tendency was to speak first in a decision-making conversation because she thought the team would appreciate knowing what they should do. However, while speaking first might speed up decision-making, it made team members less likely to share their own good ideas. What they didn't do was incorporate any of those specific behaviors or practices into their performance goals. In other words, they didn't set up any ways to measure those practices. Reasons why will be covered in the next chapter, which is about knowing the organization you are part of. In the meantime, if a leader doesn't have a way to measure actions with individuals and/or the team, they won't know how they are doing or if their efforts are having the impact they want. See chapter seven for more on setting goals and measuring success.

PRACTICES FOR BUILDING INCLUSION ON TEAMS

The most common practice that leaders mentioned during our interviews was listening to the perspectives of many people, not just a few. Those who named this behavior stated they were either already doing so or realized they needed to do it more often. I would have liked to interview employees who worked for them to validate what was said, but that was beyond the scope of my research.

I found several nuggets. One interviewee, Stephen, told me that after attending an unconscious bias class, he realized he kept giving assignments to the same people on his team over and over, based on their past performance. Stephen recognized something else, though. He said, "I gave things to people because of how well they perform, and I realized that . . . I was taking the path of least resistance, or that has the highest degree of success. It was my unconscious bias that was driving a behavior that was not helping the team."

Stephen wasn't necessarily thinking of what others on the team might be able or willing to do. He saw that, at best, his actions were not helping other team members grow or develop. At worst, he was risking his team members burning out.

Another interviewee, Kareen, admitted, "I have to monitor my behavior. I tend to expect that everyone has the same energy and creativity about the goals that I do." Not surprisingly, she would get frustrated and critical when people didn't have the same approach. This is a huge admission. To expect a team to collectively take the same approach as a leader might mean amplifying the strengths of that approach, but also means a potential car wreck of an outcome if that approach is overused or if a new situation occurs that requires a pivot. Acknowledging that other people have different energies and ways to approach goals means she can now tap into their creativity and potential for new solutions.

Then there was Levi, who purposely asked for his team members' opinions. "I want to help somebody and talk through an issue with them . . . to get their perspective . . . I give them the opportunity to express how they actually feel." Although he used the word "feel," in the context of the interview, he was describing meetings where he asked people what they thought was a preferred course of action, and he made a point to speak last.

Revisiting Self-Awareness

Amy Edmondson wrote in 2012 about organizational success through leading effective teams rather than creating effective teams.[11] One strategy for leaders is to encourage team members to reflect on their ways of working. To do so requires that leaders reflect on how they interact with their teams and be willing to adjust their own leadership style to what the team needs. It can be humbling but worth it.

Self-Awareness and Empathy

We all have biases. Self-awareness is a prerequisite to understanding our personal and professional biases. Research shows the value of empathy in working to foster individual learning (again, see the previous chapter). Individuals must first develop self-awareness. From self-awareness comes the possibility of empathy and openness to learning about others, which allows individuals to apply these empathic insights in the systems they inhabit.[12]

For example, several studies of medical and dental students included a focus on empathy and self-reflection as two elements of professionalism and as necessary components of their education programs.[13] I found in my research that self-reflection is a prerequisite for empathy. It does not seem bidirectional to me, nor could I find any research showing that it works in the opposite direction. Empathy is not a prerequisite for self-reflection.

Self-Reflection

I came across the concept of perspective-taking during my research. It's a fancy name for "perceiving a situation or understanding a concept from an alternative point of view, such as that of another individual."[14] Taking another's point of view can enhance self-reflection. I also discovered that multiple techniques were effective for increasing perspective-taking and enhancing self-reflection. Specifically, journaling or writing blogs was foundational to self-reflection, as was sharing those reflections in small, supportive peer group sessions.[15] In one study, self-reflection as a path to empathy was more likely to occur through the act of taking another person's perspective.[16]

Here's an example of how perspective can enhance a mentoring relationship in both directions. I was a mentor to a younger woman who was developing as a leader. She described feeling a sense of loss when two members of her leadership hierarchy left the company. I took her perspective for a moment, remembering my own sense of loss when a trusted leader had left the organization. I felt empathy for what she was experiencing. I referred to that memory when I advised her to start now to build a network intentionally, over time, which I had not done for myself until much later in my career. I then shared with her how valuable our mentoring relationship was for me because it was an opportunity to reflect on what has been most helpful and important in my own journey.

Leaders influence the organizations they work in while the organization influences them. This is a bidirectional relationship, and I discuss it further in chapter four. Here, I'm focusing on the interactions that leaders have every day with one or more members of a team. As previously mentioned, when leaders practice self-reflection and make meaning of their own philosophies, biases, and behaviors, they can more likely make adjustments in how they interact with their teams. It's also important to be curious and open to how to change to be an effective leader, but how motivated does someone need to be to make changes? This was a question I wanted to discuss in my interviews.

Motivation and Inclusion

This seems like a good time to explain what I mean by "motivation." A concise definition I use is that motivation is an internal or external driving force that initiates, sustains, and directs behavior toward achieving a goal or fulfilling a need. Quite simply, it is what moves us to take action.[17] But the topic is far from simple.

Motivation has been a key subject in fields such as psychology, business, education, sports, and personal development for over a century. There are likely tens of thousands of books about motivation, from textbooks to self-help guides to business books. Some famous books from different eras include Abraham Maslow's *Motivation and Personality* (which introduced the hierarchy of needs), Frederick Herzberg and colleagues' *The Motivation to Work*, and Daniel Pink's *Drive*. Add academic and professional articles and the number is even higher. Thousands of articles are published annually across academic journals in psychology, business, education, and other fields. Major psychology and business databases contain hundreds of thousands of articles that explore various aspects of motivation theory, including intrinsic versus extrinsic motivation, behavioral theories, and more-recent models such as self-determination theory. You get the idea. A few more details about different types of motivation might help here.

For my dissertation, I found motivation theories that explained why people feel something is worth doing. I was happy to learn about these because I have often wondered about my own motivational drive to be a better person but am concerned that my highly competitive streak and desire for praise from others could be derailing me. To provide more context, I'll describe two types of motivation. Extrinsic motivation is based on external factors or rewards, such as money, praise, or avoiding punishment. For instance, for most of my career, I was motivated to do my best work so that my immediate manager would praise me. I constantly needed that feedback; when it came, I was motivated to try even harder to get more praise, and when I didn't get it, I was crushed.

Conversely, intrinsic motivation comes from within an individual and is tied to personal enjoyment, a sense of pride in overcoming a challenge, or learning a new skill. What is significant is unique for each individual. For example, in writing this book, I was motivated by the sense that I am contributing to other people's learning. I feel good about the commitment of time and effort I've made to writing over a period of several months. I believe I'm contributing to a larger community. I do not need anyone to tell me I did a good job.

By recognizing and leveraging these different types of motivation, leaders can create a more dynamic and motivated workforce.

In my research, I first wanted to know if leaders would perceive that achieving performance goals for inclusion was important, which would suggest intrinsic motivation, or useful, which indicates a preference for extrinsic motivation. And if so, would they be more likely to commit to the goal in the first place, to persist in making progress on the goal, and to spend mental effort to be successful?

The leaders I interviewed overwhelmingly believed that incorporating inclusionary practices into their goals is important. It also became clear that they did not make a distinction between something being important versus being useful. This may sound like splitting hairs, and you might wonder if it really matters if something is perceived as important rather than useful. It's a fair question. A lot of what we are talking about in this book is recognition of nuances that might not be clear to others but which you see as helpful.

By setting clear team norms, using assessments to discover communication styles, celebrating diverse contributions, and fostering psychological safety, you can strengthen both cognitive and affective trust. Another important aspect was how leaders can leverage empathy, self-awareness, and inclusive practices—such as actively seeking input and recognizing different preferences—to unite team members around common goals. At the same time, as much as employees want you to know their individual strengths and skills and to take seriously their points of view, prior expertise, and background, they would appreciate that you know what motivates them individually.

When you can understand what drives each person on the team—whether it's career growth, work-life balance, or passion for specific types of projects—you can create conditions for their success that show you value and support them. Ultimately, knowing your team, individually and collectively, helps you create a sense of belonging, boost engagement, and leverage the collective power of diverse perspectives for better, more sustainable business results.

CHAPTER THREE SUMMARY

THREE KEY POINTS

1. Assessments help individuals understand themselves and team members understand one another better, but they need to be treated as the means to an end, not an end in themselves.

2. Tuckman's model is a helpful framework for knowing how to adjust to what a team needs at different stages of its journey.

3. Motivation theories explain why people respond differently to rewards—some value achievement; others seek tangible benefits.

THREE REFLECTIVE QUESTIONS

1. How well do I know each team member's strengths, preferences, and motivations?

2. What is one thing I can do differently, or what can I start doing, stop doing, or do more often?

3. What do I need to do to tailor my leadership approach to meet the needs of my team at their current stage of development?

THREE ACTIONS YOU CAN TAKE

1. Conduct a team assessment: Use a well-suited tool, such as MBTI, DiSC, or CliftonStrengths, to uncover individual and team preferences. Facilitate a debrief session to encourage open discussions about differences and to foster a shared understanding of how to work together more effectively.

2. Establish or revisit team norms: Collaboratively create norms that emphasize inclusion, respect, and collaboration. For example, introduce norms such as "take space and make space" to balance contributions from all team members, ensuring everyone's voice is heard. This is especially important any time team membership changes.

3. Recognize and leverage motivational drivers: Identify what motivates each team member, whether intrinsic (attainment value) or extrinsic (utility value). Use this insight to align tasks and development opportunities with their unique drivers, showing that you value and support their individual goals.

CHAPTER FOUR

Know Your Organization

When I was a girl, my friends and I played double Dutch, a skipping rope game that required rhythm, coordination, and perfect timing. Two people turned ropes in sync while a third had to watch, anticipate the flow, and leap in at just the right moment. Once inside, the jumper had to stay attuned to the pace, height, and rhythm of the ropes, adjusting their movements while the rope-turners subtly shifted to maintain balance.

Organizations are far more complex than a childhood game, but the dynamics of interdependence hold true. Just as the jumper must understand the system before engaging, leaders need to assess the structures and rhythms of their organizations before diving into inclusion work. The more you understand these moving parts, the better you can create and sustain an inclusive workplace. Doing so can impact employees' job performances, creativity, and sense of empowerment, while also influencing how they identify with the groups they are part of.[1]

In this chapter, I describe two ways to better understand

your organization. I'll share them one at a time, including the basic concepts; give you a few examples and stories from my research; and explain how you can apply these concepts as part of your strategy to build or sustain an inclusive environment.

ORGANIZATIONS AS SYSTEMS

Organizations operate as complex systems where multiple components must align for efficiency and for any meaningful change. The Star Model, developed by Jay Galbraith, provides a framework to diagnose organizational challenges and design strategies that consider all key elements.[2] Many companies develop inclusion initiatives without checking whether their structures, processes, or incentives actually support them. The Star Model helps ensure alignment—because without it, even the best intentions can falter.

Using the model is not as simple as showing it to a leader and assuming they will embrace it. After more than a dozen years of bringing the framework into my work, I've learned that it does not matter if I think it is a terrific diagnostic and design tool. Leaders still want practical applications. First, I have to know the business problems they care about, and I cover how to do that, and why it is important, in the next chapter. Typically the source of the problem can be traced to gaps in performance against a goal involving people, processes, reward systems, a strategic plan, or the power structures. All of these are connected as shown in the Star Model. Any time even one of the elements are changed, the others are all impacted as well.

To learn more about the Star Model and its use in organizations, I highly recommend "Designing Dynamic Organizations: A Hands-On Guide for Leaders at All Levels."[3] This model consists of five key components:

direction

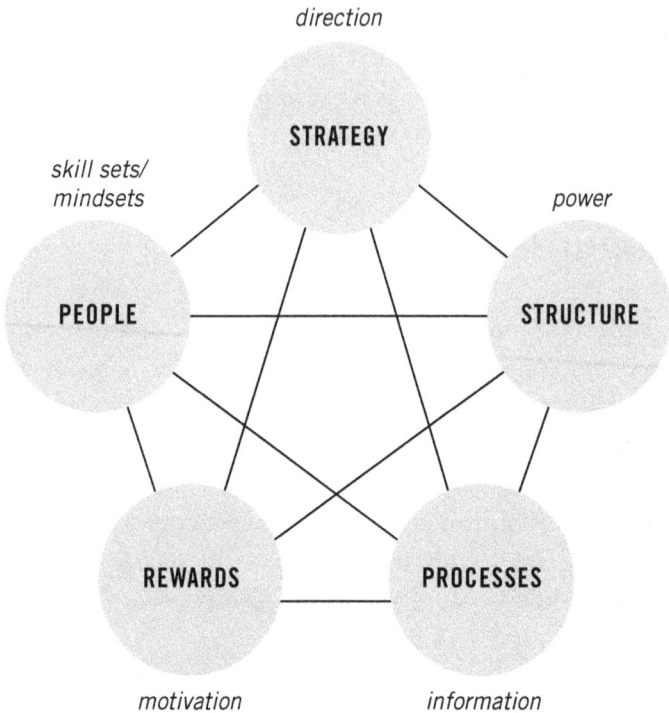

skill sets/   power
mindsets

Figure 2. The Star Model.

Strategy: Incorporating Inclusion

Get the strategy right, and everything else flows easier. Why? Strategy is all about the organization's direction and long-term goals. Many companies struggle with strategy for various reasons. They write goals or action plans, which are fine for a short-term focus but not the same as designing proactive or innovative ways to win new markets or outperform competitors. But strategy is critical, foundational, and essential for a company's success. And as a company develops its long-term goals and direction, it must incorporate inclusion, which is much more powerful if built into a company's strategy.

As you consider the strategic direction your company is

taking, you can begin to build inclusive practices right away. For example, you can track and measure the degree to which you proactively seek input from all parts of your organization or department when making a business plan for the year. Harvesting the knowledge and experience of others, especially those colleagues working in other parts of the business, increases the likelihood of seeing unique ways to go after new markets or better understand customers' points of view.

One simple yet powerful way to build inclusion into your strategy is to seek input from those who see the organization with fresh eyes—your new hires. Too often, when a new employee offers an idea, the response is a dismissive "that won't work here" or "we tried that once—it didn't work." Reactions like these don't just stifle innovation; they also silence people before they've even found their voice.

Instead, consider that you hired these people to leverage their expertise. What do they know, see, or do that you've stopped noticing? What assumptions does your team make without questioning? Listening to these perspectives strengthens strategic decision-making while reinforcing from day one that every voice matters.

If you don't have input on organization-wide strategy, you can still embed inclusion into your team's strategy by setting clear priorities. Start by crafting an inclusive vision statement, ensuring that your strategic goals reflect a commitment to diverse perspectives, and tracking progress through meaningful inclusion metrics such as engagement scores and retention rates. Bonus points when you develop it with input from across your group, rather than taking a half-day off-site meeting to develop it with the same chosen few.

Structure: Designing for Representation and Inclusion

Structure describes how the organization is designed, including its hierarchy and reporting relationships. Here's an insight based on my experience: Leaders often assume restructuring will solve inefficiencies, but no organizational structure is a perfect fix. Every model enables certain ways of working while creating new limitations—and if leaders focus only on efficiency or hierarchy, they might miss how structure affects inclusion.

Look at your team's structure and ask: Who is missing from key decisions? Who has influence, and who doesn't? Designing inclusive teams means ensuring diverse perspectives are represented, not just at entry levels but across leadership roles. Even if you don't control organizational design, you can influence inclusion by forming cross-functional teams, elevating underrepresented voices in decision-making, and ensuring hierarchy doesn't stifle participation.

Processes: Limitless Opportunities for Inclusion

Countless workflows, processes, and systems connect different parts of the organization. These include the flow of work and how management objectives get set or decisions get made. Processes might or might not be documented, but you should be able to see evidence of how they work. For example, knowledge documents describe information such as policies or practices, while job aids or manuals explain procedures or the "how-to."

If the processes that govern hiring, promotions, and talent development aren't designed with inclusion in mind, they may inadvertently exclude certain groups. For example, in many organizations, hiring processes prioritize familiarity—leaders unconsciously favoring candidates they already know, giving only a cursory interview to others.

You have many daily routines in your role, including decision-making. Take a moment to think about how it happens for you and your team: Does decision-making involve clear, transparent criteria so employees understand how opportunities are allocated? When people feel included in decision-making, they contribute more fully, driving both better outcomes and stronger commitment. Start now to experiment with adding inclusion to your daily, weekly, and monthly routines. Pause here to consider just two ideas:

- Implement inclusive decision-making: Introduce practices such as consensus-building and consultative processes to ensure diverse perspectives are considered.
- Foster transparency: Share decision-making criteria and outcomes openly to build trust and accountability.

Rewards: Recognize and Reinforce Inclusive Behavior

Rewards signal what the organization values, yet many leaders assume pay and promotions are the only meaningful incentives. While those matter, recognition also comes through day-to-day reinforcement—from acknowledging contributions in meetings to celebrating inclusive behaviors.

Leaders can embed inclusion into performance reviews, ensuring that feedback considers not just individual achievements but also how leaders foster inclusion within their teams. Formal recognition programs can highlight employees who champion inclusive collaboration. Even small actions, such as publicly acknowledging who helped drive success, reinforce the fact that inclusion is not just a metric—it's a core leadership value.

As a leader, you might not have a lot of leeway regarding compensation. Pay ranges, salary changes, and promotions are often decided at certain times of the year and/or by a committee of senior leaders. You might have some control over nonmonetary rewards. For example, one employee might appreciate a day off with pay as a thank-you for a job well done on a project, while another might like to attend a conference in their professional area of interest.

In addition to understanding what you can do to ensure you're being inclusive in how you reward employees, check out how the organization rewards inclusion, if at all. Are managers expected to have at least one goal based on inclusionary practices? Do performance reviews include assessments of how well leaders are fostering an inclusive environment? Does the organization reward inclusionary practices? If behaviors and outcomes on any topic are not measured, it is difficult to understand how they are considered important and how they will be rewarded. If there are no expectations, can you choose one thing that you can do, such as celebrating instances of inclusion where appropriate? Part of being inclusive is understanding what kind of recognition would appeal to someone and what would be uncomfortable—like doing it in public versus privately.

People: Develop Inclusive Capabilities

The people element focuses on hiring, developing, and retaining talent. Its focus is the skills and capabilities that everyone needs to be successful now and in the future. As a leader, you can prioritize building your workforce in such a way that it reflects the diversity of your customer base and equips employees with the skills to thrive in an inclusive culture. You can take actions all the way through the employee life cycle— the stages of an employee's time with a company—beginning with hiring diverse employees but also providing mentoring, allyship, training, and development opportunities that allow everyone to thrive.

Also be aware that this work is never finished. Employees

look around them and look up, searching for people like them in leadership or desirable positions, and if they don't see them, they are more likely to leave. This has been proven time and time again in surveys and research. Try the following ways to embed inclusion into how you develop people around you:

- Develop others for an inclusion mindset: Provide ongoing training on unconscious bias and cultural competence. Beyond training, notice and acknowledge when you see examples of people operating in an inclusive way.
- Mentor underrepresented talent: Establish mentorship and sponsorship programs to support career growth for underrepresented employees.
- Prioritize retention: Use engagement surveys to understand employee concerns and address systemic issues. Better yet, try conducting "stay interviews," an excellent concept Beverly Kaye and Sharon Jordan-Evans explain as a guide for proactive, meaningful conversations about what makes employees want to stay and what might cause them to leave—so you can take action before it's too late.[4]

Note: I am only recommending actions I have tried myself, and when I conducted stay interviews with a team I led, several employees expressed appreciation that I was doing this. They enjoyed the conversation. I learned a lot about their individual preferences and, in a couple of cases, made some adjustments to how we worked together.

By ensuring alignment across these five dimensions, you can do a lot to shape an organization that delivers on its goals. When applied to inclusion, the Star Model helps leaders build systems that embed inclusive principles into the organization's DNA.

ORGANIZATIONAL CULTURE: NAVIGATING THE INVISIBLE FORCES THAT SHAPE BEHAVIOR

While frameworks such as the Star Model provide the tangible landscape for inclusion, culture plays an equally vital yet less visible role. Edgar Schein, a renowned expert on organizational culture, defines it as "the set of shared values, beliefs, and norms that guide how people behave within an organization."[5]

I was fortunate enough to have been in a seminar Ed hosted in the mid-1990s. As a shiny new organization-development consultant, I was spellbound by his stories of his work. Thirty years later, his practical, thorough description of the three levels of culture that shape how organizations function still resonates as the masterclass that it was.[6] These learned patterns become deeply ingrained and are often taken for granted. In brief, here's how they apply and how you can act on them.

Artifacts: Visible Signs of Inclusion

Artifacts are the tangible elements of culture, such as dress codes, office layouts, or the language people use in meetings. These visible cues signal who belongs and what is valued. For example, if leadership meetings are consistently dominated by the same few perspectives, it suggests that certain voices are more influential than others. Conversely, you would recognize an inclusive environment when diverse perspectives are visible in teams, company materials, and workplace celebrations.

Actionable Steps

- **Diversify symbols** to reflect the range of identities in office spaces, on digital platforms, and in marketing materials.

- **Celebrate broadly** by recognizing holidays and milestones such as Pride Month, Black History Month, and Diwali, not just those that are obvious or mainstream.
- **Review policies** to ensure workplace guidelines (e.g., dress codes, remote work) meet diverse needs.

Espoused Values: Beyond Statements

Espoused values are the official statements about what an organization values, such as diversity and inclusion. But if these stated values don't align with daily behavior, people will know. Are inclusion goals clearly communicated and embraced at all levels of the organization, or are they merely a checkbox exercise? You can allow inclusion to thrive by ensuring these values are not only aspirational but also reflected in daily actions.

Actionable Steps

- **Live your values** by consistently seeking different perspectives and fostering open dialogue.
- **Use feedback tools** such as a 360-degree review, and lead by example by going first in sharing insights and improvements.
- **Communicate your messages of inclusion** in meetings, emails, chat spaces, and other means of connection.

Underlying Assumptions: Unspoken Workplace Norms

Unconscious beliefs and norms drive behavior. For instance, an organization may espouse a commitment to diversity but operate on the assumption that the most valuable employees are those who fit a traditional mold. These hidden assumptions often create the biggest barriers to inclusion. Deep, sustainable change requires challenging these hidden assumptions, and as leaders, we need courage and stamina to show the way.

Actionable Steps

- **Identify hidden biases** through surveys, focus groups, and regular discussions. If you are part of a leadership team, communicate what you and your peers are noticing in your meetings. Be the first to show vulnerability and empathy.
- **Challenge outdated norms** that reinforce rigid expectations of how work gets done, such as long or rigid work hours, or the assumption that face time is the only way to be productive.
- **Encourage dialogue** where employees can openly share concerns and ideas. Ensuring people have ways to exchange and appreciate perspectives is a positive first step toward an inclusive environment, especially in learning spaces such as workshops.

Schein's work highlights an essential truth: Culture is not just what an organization says—it's what it does. As leaders, we have a responsibility to examine and shape both visible and invisible aspects of culture. By addressing artifacts, aligning stated values with actions, and uncovering hidden assumptions, we can create an environment where inclusion is more than a goal—it's the way we operate every day.

INTEGRATING THE STAR MODEL AND SCHEIN'S FRAMEWORK

I realize I've put two different models in front of you and only touched the surface of each one. It can be confusing to know where to go next or what to pay attention to. Both models are equally important, and here's how they complement each other: Integrating the Star Model and Schein's cultural insights enables you to address both the structural and cultural dimensions of inclusion and to understand how the tangible and intangible can work together. Consider them two pillars of support: the Star Model provides the systems-level blueprint, while Schein's framework ensures these systems are rooted in authentic cultural change. With both, you can:

Link Strategy to Culture

You can check that the inclusion strategy outlined in the Star Model is grounded in an understanding of existing cultural dynamics in your department or organization. For example, if your organization's culture values innovation, the inclusion strategy can emphasize how including multiple perspectives drives creativity.

Align Structures with Values

Do the structural elements of the Star Model, such as cross-functional teams, reflect and reinforce espoused values such as collaboration and respect? If not, you can involve team members in diagnosing reasons for the gap, then align on ways to close it.

Drive Cultural Change Through Processes

Processes designed to standardize equity, such as inclusive hiring practices, can be paired with efforts to shift underlying assumptions about merit and competence. Often, focusing on business problems can lead to understanding flawed or no-longer-helpful processes. One of Edgar Schein's core insights about culture is that leaders "should not focus on culture change. Focus on a business problem."[7] More on this in the next chapter.

Reward Cultural Alignment

Reward systems can be used not only to incentivize inclusive outcomes but also to recognize efforts to align the behaviors you seek with the organization's cultural values.

Empower Other People to Lead Cultural Change

Develop and empower employees at all levels to act as cultural stewards, using tools and systems designed through the Star Model to embed inclusive practices in their daily work. When I say cultural steward, I mean someone who is attending to and nurturing the culture, which can sometimes mean tackling problematic conditions in the environment. It's far easier to tackle the problem, which can be defined, measured, and managed, than the culture, so much of which is intangible, hard to measure, and bigger than any one person. Yet individuals at all levels influence and are influenced by their environment. Leaders and employees alike are not just shaped by their organization's systems and culture—they also actively shape them. This dynamic interplay between individuals, the systems they operate within, and the culture they contribute to can be a powerful lever for change.

In the journey toward building inclusive organizations, it is easy to focus on the larger systems and cultural frameworks that shape behavior. Every organization is a living ecosystem where the actions, decisions, and behaviors of its members interact with systems and culture in a continuous feedback loop. However, individual actions are equally vital, as they continuously interact with and influence the environment.

THE CONNECTION AMONG INDIVIDUALS, SYSTEMS, AND CULTURE

Let's explore the connection among individuals, systems, and culture and how individuals at all levels can influence their environment. I'll continue to refer to principles that align with the Galbraith Star Model and Edgar Schein's insights. By integrating these perspectives, I'll show that fostering inclusion is both a systemic and deeply personal endeavor. This interplay works as follows:

The choices leaders and employees make every day influence systems (e.g., processes and rewards) and reinforce or challenge cultural norms. It might not feel true or like big changes are happening, but over time, a few or many employees can cause a definite shift.

One personal example comes to mind. I worked for years at a small computer-technology company that was eventually acquired by a much larger tech company known for a very different culture. At first, it didn't feel like much had changed. We kept doing our work, and the larger company mostly left us alone. But gradually, a few leaders from our original company were promoted into senior roles. Their leadership styles reflected the culture we'd come from—collaborative, curious, and human—and those traits were clearly valued. That told me something important: Different leadership styles could succeed, even in a much bigger system.

A few years later, our now-very-large tech company acquired another firm with an entirely different product focus. This time, the shift was more noticeable. Within a year, meetings were filled with new voices from the acquired company—experienced professionals who brought fresh ideas and ways of thinking. Slowly but surely, their influence was felt. The company grew, not just in size but in perspective. Cultural change doesn't always announce itself with a big splash. Sometimes, it's more like a tide—it creeps in, and one day you realize the shore looks different.

Systems Guide Behavior

Organizational structures, processes, and policies provide the tangible scaffolding within which individuals operate, influencing their actions and decisions. Such concrete elements are in balance with the less visible shared beliefs, values, and assumptions of the organization, shaping how people behave and what actions are deemed acceptable or innovative. This mutual influence means that every individual has the potential to either reinforce or reshape their environment, depending on how they interact with these elements.

Leveraging Personal Influence for Inclusion

Knowing that behaviors and decisions can have a ripple effect throughout an organization might seem overwhelming. How can one person affect an entire culture? On the other hand, it can be empowering. Similar to being a role model (as leaders, we are role models—people look to us—whether we choose so or not), we can be intentional and proactive in our interactions with systems and culture, and we can be catalysts for inclusion. Here's how this works in practical terms.

BEHAVIOR: INDIVIDUAL ACTIONS AS CATALYSTS FOR CHANGE

Every action a leader or employee takes sends a signal to the broader organization about what is valued and accepted. For instance:

- Listening to diverse voices: When a leader actively
  seeks input from employees who might otherwise
  be overlooked, they set an example for inclusive
  decision-making. It can be difficult to listen before
  speaking, especially at the pace at which businesses
  operate. Francis, another senior leader I interviewed, shared what listening to others did for him.
  He stated, "I'm benefiting from giving the person
  the benefit of the doubt. . . . The practice I have
  tried to adopt is to ask their opinion rather than
  state my own." Francis realized that by making it a
  habit to listen to others, he himself would benefit.

- Challenging bias: Speaking up when encounter-
  ing exclusionary practices demonstrates courage
  and reinforces the organization's commitment
  to inclusion. Francis shared a poignant example of challenging bias. He recounted standing
  up in a team meeting to declare that comments
  being made to a person of color on the team were
  unacceptable and that perhaps the person making
  those comments did not belong in the department. In telling this story, Francis recalled that
  the questionable comments were considered "a
  joke" by those making them, and he wanted to be
  clear that he would not tolerate even misguided
  humor. Afterward, several people thanked him
  for his emphatic statement. It's possible that the
  action Francis took will motivate others to speak
  up in a similar way in the future, should the occa-
  sion arise.

- Celebrating wins: Recognizing and rewarding
  inclusive behaviors in others creates momentum
  for broader cultural change.

Empower Employees to Act as Change Agents

While leaders hold significant power to influence systems and culture, all employees have the potential to contribute to an inclusive environment. Organizations can empower individuals by:

- Providing tools for action: Training sessions on inclusive behaviors, workshops on bias awareness, and clear reporting channels for concerns equip employees to act.
- Recognizing grassroots efforts: Rewarding employees who take initiative in fostering inclusion— whether through mentoring, organizing cultural events, or proposing process improvements— encourages others to do the same.
- Creating safe spaces: Forums, employee resource groups, and open-door policies give employees platforms to express ideas, share concerns, and influence change. An example of how to create safe spaces comes from interviewee Valerie. I asked about practices that leaders used to be inclusive. Valerie described a habit of listening as a way to "create a safe space of a respectful, open environment . . . Everyone can express their opinions."

Interestingly, Ben (remember him from the introduction?) described the effect of not listening: "If you have a leader who cannot listen, they are not connecting with the person they're talking to, and they're missing an opportunity."

To operate like Francis, Valerie, and Ben, consider your level of engagement with systems, culture, and individuals. You might not do all these at the same time, but attending to each of them regularly will help maintain that balance. All action with no reflection can mean depending on luck to have the impact you want, while reflection without action is ineffective too.

THE INCLUSIVE ECOSYSTEM: A LEADER'S CALL TO ACTION

Organizations are never in a resting state. They are constantly shifting and evolving based on the connections and dependencies among individuals and systems.[8] By understanding this interdependence, any one of us, especially in the role of a leader, can take deliberate steps to foster inclusion at every level. Every choice matters:

- A process reimagined can remove barriers for underrepresented employees.
- A courageous conversation can challenge outdated cultural norms.
- A single inclusive behavior can inspire a ripple effect throughout the organization.

If Jay Galbraith's Star Model is a way for leaders to shape how an organization delivers on its goals, and Edgar Schein's insights on organizational culture provide a lens for understanding the underlying beliefs, values, and assumptions that shape workplace behavior, combining the two to amplify and embed inclusionable practices is a repeatable approach that can lead to better business results and enhanced employee engagement.

Inclusive leadership is not about perfection—it's about consistent, intentional efforts to create an environment where every individual feels seen, valued, and empowered. By using tools like the Star Model to design inclusive systems and applying insights into cultural dynamics, leaders can catalyze meaningful change. Just as importantly, by recognizing their own role in shaping the environment, they can inspire others to do the same, ensuring that inclusion is not just a goal but a shared responsibility.

CHAPTER FOUR SUMMARY

THREE KEY POINTS

1. Building and sustaining an inclusive environment requires a dual focus on systems and culture. Taken together, these two frameworks can help you notice and diagnose the tangible and intangible elements of your environment. In doing so, you can take concrete steps to build inclusive systems and cultures.

2. The Star Model provides leaders with a practical framework to understand, diagnose, and design systems that can embed inclusive principles into the organization's strategy, structure, processes, rewards, and people practices. Meanwhile, Edgar Schein's insights on organizational culture offer a deeper understanding of the beliefs and assumptions that shape behavior.

3. You can observe, diagnose, and act on your own part of the organization. You do not have to wait until a consultant or senior leader does so. In fact, you know better than anyone, along with your team, what is both tangible and intangible in your organization. Taking the time to reflect, discuss, and align on what is happening at and below the surface gives you all the data you need to act.

THREE REFLECTIVE QUESTIONS

1. How would a visitor to my organization describe our culture?

2. What artifacts, espoused values, and underlying assumptions describe our culture?

3. Who else should I be discussing this with?

THREE ACTIONS YOU CAN TAKE

1. Regularly solicit feedback from employees about their experiences. Listen to their input with empathy and without judgment, excuses, or explanations.

2. Based on the feedback you get, take visible actions to address concerns. If that feels like a big project, decide on one action you know you can do for at least thirty days, to experiment and learn.

3. Role model embedding inclusion in your organization. Champion inclusion publicly and privately. Speak about inclusion as a strategic priority linked to business objectives. Do it in public forums, and ensure that private actions—such as decisions in hiring, promotions, or resource allocation—align with these commitments.

CHAPTER FIVE

Know the Business Problem

I almost dropped out of my doctoral program in my first semester. I am not a quitter, but a course with the deceptively simple title of "Framing" was a humbling experience that made me rethink decades of how I had viewed some basic concepts. The course required students to frame or define a "macro" (meaning universal) problem to be solved in a clear and succinct manner. It was only three paragraphs! What is the problem, how do I know it's a problem, and what is the importance of solving the problem? Simple enough, right?

No. I was not right three times out of three. My instructor's comments were that each of my attempts to define a problem were "a solution looking for a problem."

I was confused and irritated. With over twenty years of experience in leadership and organization development, how could I be getting this wrong?

Then two things happened. First, I remembered having this same feeling of dog paddling in strange water during the first semester of my master's program many years ago. The instructor had told the class repeatedly that our task in the assignments was not to leap into action to solve what we thought was the problem. Instead, we were meant to conduct a thorough diagnosis of an organization, including its strategy, performance goals against results, and several other criteria. We would be graded on how well we were able to diagnose what was going on in the case studies.

Diagnosis seemed to be the opposite of what most of us had learned in our various companies. Who had time to sit around and talk about what might be the problem? Acting quickly and decisively to identify and solve problems was what got noticed and rewarded. Gradually, I realized that it's easy to take action but difficult to properly diagnose the right problem.

Back to my doctoral program from a few years ago. The second thing that happened was that I got curious. What was this new-to-me way of thinking and writing? How could I turn my frustration into something useful? I grumpily decided to follow instructions instead of trying to be right.

I really listened, for a change. This time, my instructor's advice flipped a switch for me. "Any time you find yourself saying there is a lack of something," he told the class, "it means you have a solution that you want to apply to the situation." Apparently, I was not the only one struggling. My instructor said I needed proof, such as data or evidence, that something was, in fact, a problem. Without that, it may not actually be a problem, which meant I was defining the "problem" based on my own experience. And that meant I really didn't understand the problem; I was forcing a situation to meet my own preferences for how I solved problems.

People complained about that course for the rest of our program, but it was one of the biggest gifts I received. That instructor became my dissertation advisor and chair, and we worked well together because I saw the value of what he was doing to help and guide me.

DEFINING THE PROBLEM

Now it's over to you. What problem are you trying to solve? Nowadays, I routinely ask this question at the start of a meeting or a project kickoff. And two things can happen. Sometimes everyone starts talking at once, in an attempt to be the first to state what they think is obvious. The other way the conversation goes is that people get very quiet as they realize they have not asked this question yet.

It is critical to know the problem. Consider the words of Kimberlé Crenshaw in an excellent TED talk from 2016.[1] She describes how multiple forms of exclusion, such as being both a woman and an African American, can intersect. The double exclusion of race and gender led Dr. Crenshaw to create the term "intersectionality." Until she did so, there was no name for the problem of double exclusion. As Crenshaw pointed out, "When there's no name for a problem, you can't see a problem. And when you can't see a problem, you pretty much can't solve it."

Problems often seem obvious because we solve dozens of them every day. But that's where we can go wrong—assuming we know the problem before we've fully explored it.

After more than three decades in corporate environments, I believe that most people come to work each day ready—often eager—to solve problems. It's how our brains are wired. Long ago, noticing a threat and acting quickly was how we stayed alive. In today's workplace, we've swapped predators for performance issues, but the instinct remains: Spot the problem, act fast, move on. That same instinct can lead us to jump into familiar solutions without taking time to understand what the real problem is. We're rewarded for speed, volume, and visible impact—so it's no wonder we rush. But sometimes, in our hurry to fix, we miss the chance to really see and understand what's going on. And many problems I've dealt with are not what appear on the surface, but something underneath. Here's a personal example of how I was trying to solve the wrong problem (and it was the same problem with slightly different variations) for several years.

I left two jobs in a row for the same reason, and it took me until recently to realize I had been trying to solve the wrong problem both times. Even worse, I failed to see that I actually was the problem. Well, not me personally, but my way of thinking about these situations.

The reason I left two jobs in succession is that I thought the leaders I was working with just didn't understand what it took to be a great leader. The same pattern emerged in both situations: I tried to build relationships with the leaders I was supporting because I truly believed that before we could do great work together, we had to have a strong relationship built on trust, respect, and shared values. When they didn't reciprocate in the way I was expecting, I began to judge them as not being great leaders. I believed I could only be effective if we had a positive working relationship based on knowing each other. I had (I realize now) a myopic view of the way things should be, and my narrow view of the best way to work together meant I didn't see I needed to flex, to try other approaches, to consider that my way of working was not bringing value to them in ways that mattered. In short, I was spending no time at all on self-reflection. I thought that by leaving behind the leaders I found lacking in character or commitment, I would be able to find new, better leaders who understood what *was* important.

Several years later, an interaction with a senior leader finally opened my eyes, my mind, and my heart to the need for me to change. I heard through the grapevine at work that a leader I had never met (it was a big company!) was planning some big changes in his organization, and it sounded to me like he would need my help in making these changes happen. I had nothing to lose by offering my help, because I already had plenty of work supporting other leaders as an internal organization-development consultant. I was already not working with him, so even if he said no, I wouldn't be any worse off than I already was.

Through a colleague, I got an introduction to the leader and nervously prepared for a first meeting. How could we work together when we didn't know each other? I knew I had only one chance to get him to work with me; he was known for preferring to work with outside consultants when he needed help. As the leader began to talk about what he wanted to do, I became energized. He was describing things I was doing with other leaders in the same organization. "I can help you with what you want to do," I blurted out, even though I didn't know how I would do this work with someone I didn't have an established relationship with.

"You can?" he asked. He seemed open to the idea.

We discussed a few next steps and agreed on some meetings and timelines. Over the next six months, I worked with a task force he created; we reported back to him on a regular basis, and in a capstone three-day meeting I facilitated most of, we accomplished everything he had asked for. Eventually, he opened up to me a bit more, and I worked with him and his leadership team a few more times. When I moved into another part of the business, it was to learn about new functions and roles, not because I thought the leaders didn't get it. I had evidence I could build relationships by doing great work with someone else. And I finally understood that the problem was never that I had to build relationships first; that was just a preference. The problem was that I had failed to take the perspective of the people I was trying to support. No wonder I was misdiagnosing the problems I was trying to solve.

A GAP-ANALYSIS FRAMEWORK

You might be familiar with gap analysis. A gap is the difference between a performance target and the actual number achieved. Say you want to increase this year's sales of your product or services by 10 percent over last year. You set quarterly targets, and after the first quarter, you measure your sales against your quarterly target to determine if you have a gap. If you do, you conduct an analysis to determine the cause of the gap.

I have come across many problem-solving practices over the course of my career. I highly recommend one gap-analysis approach in particular—one I used in my research and now apply in my day-to-day consulting work. Let me introduce you to Richard E. Clark and Fred Estes's book *Turning Research into Results: A Guide to Selecting the Right Performance Solutions.* Their framework offers practical strategies to improve business performance. I'll provide a synopsis of their methodology and follow that with examples of how you might use it when analyzing potential root causes of the problem you're trying to solve. In chapter seven, we'll spend some time on implementing solutions.

UNDERSTANDING CLARK AND ESTES'S FRAMEWORK

Clark and Estes's book provides guidance on setting worthwhile performance goals and then outlines how to assess gaps in performance against the goals. Their analysis takes into account whether the gap is related to knowledge, motivation, or organizational elements, also known as KMO.[2] More on KMO later.

You can use this framework not only to set goals and diagnose performance gaps but also to project ahead to what your team or organization might need to be successful. I'm a visual learner, so I'm including a graphic I adapted from Clark and Estes's model. I used it in my dissertation, and I use it still. It helps me to consistently think through and act on all the steps, no matter what the issue is.

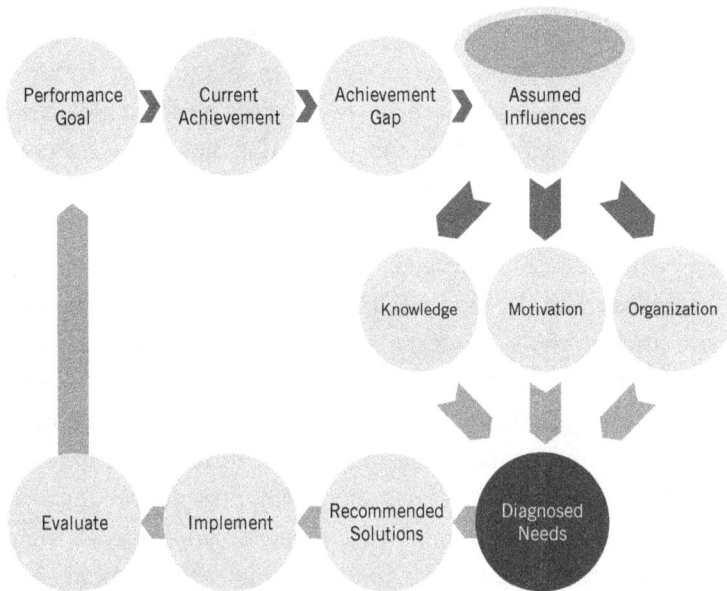

Figure 3. Clark and Estes's Gap-Analysis Model. Adapted from *Turning Research into Results: A Guide to Selecting the Right Performance Solutions* by R. E. Clark and F. Estes.

Let's examine the model in stages.

First, identify performance gaps—that is, the difference between desired performance and actual performance.

This task involves two interdependent steps. First, check that you understand or can define what successful performance looks like. It is important to understand which organizational level an expectation is coming from, because often there are "stacked" expectations. A performance expectation can start at the corporate level, then go down to a "division" level, which could have its own expectation of what *this* division would do to contribute to the corporate goal. Within a division, there are likely several functions (sales, marking, customer service), and each one sets its own expectations of how the group contributes. Is the performance expectation at the corporate level, the functions level, or the department level? (Or substitute your own organizational structure as needed.) And are those success metrics written in measurable terms?

The second step is to measure current performance. You will likely use quantitative and qualitative data to assess how current performance compares to the desired or expected standards or goals. The difference between desired and current performance is your gap.

Sounds simple, doesn't it? Yet misalignment—whether from unclear goals, miscommunication, or shifting metrics—can make performance gaps difficult to pinpoint. For example, the desired performance may not be clear to everyone. Senior leaders may have access to or set targets they assume are being communicated but aren't. Even if the desired metrics are shared, we can't assume that everyone knows what their contribution is. The further the goals and measurements get from the senior leaders who established them, the more likely it is that the goals and their measurements become unclear. In addition to that, while a goal for a company or department might be understandable, it's not always clear how individual employees can contribute to the goal or set their own goals to contribute to the bigger goals.

I have provided organization-development consulting support to various sales organizations over the years. Sales teams, of all groups, might seem to have the easiest time identifying performance gaps—if targets aren't met, the gap is clear. But shifting territories, changing quotas, and new incentive structures often complicate what should be a straightforward analysis.

One other element might help to understand the desired versus current performance metrics. Only a few pages ago, I quoted one of my professors in probably the most important course of my doctoral program: "Any time you find yourself saying there is a lack of something . . . it means you have a solution that you want to apply to the situation." It's tempting to diagnose a problem as a "lack of" something, and it's possible that after your careful analysis, there is a lack, in which case you get to be right. It is also possible that you are seeing what you want to see based on your own experience. Either way, without your due diligence, you might get pushback from others who have their own opinion about what the gap is and what the correct solution should be.

Once you've identified a gap, you will notice both an opportunity and a challenge. The opportunity is to verify or correct understanding about what makes a gap. The challenge is to look beyond the obvious contributors to a gap, including personal biases or assumptions, and dig deeper into the culture of the company if necessary. As an example, let's say a leader does not have an inclusion goal in their performance goals for their role, even though the corporate leadership says inclusion is important. I might have a bias that the gap is due to the leader not caring. But what if the leader's own boss (not the corporate leadership team) doesn't have an inclusion goal and has never mentioned it? Or what if the leader has never had to write a goal specifying inclusion metrics and has no template to follow? These are examples of having to go beyond my own bias about the leader not caring.

In the last chapter, I referenced some of Edgar Schein's many insights about culture. Do not be satisfied that the surface level or "presenting problem" is the one to solve. Instead, examine what is below the surface, and you'll likely find a more complex system of interrelated issues.

Before we move to the next step, I want to discuss the kind

of gap you might be dealing with. In my research, I knew that within one company in biotech, women and minorities were underrepresented at various leadership levels. What I didn't know was how well the company was performing against specific goals about inclusionary practices because there were none. Instead they had suggested practices, with no requirement for specific goals. I conducted a gap-analysis study, also known as needs analysis, to determine what the leaders at the company needed to do to include inclusionary practices in their performance goals.

Two questions guided me in generating the needs analysis. First, what knowledge and skills, motivation, and organizational needs existed in order for the group's leaders to incorporate at least one of the organization's DEI inclusionary practices into their performance goals? And second (after research and analysis of the data), what were my recommended solutions in order for the same leaders to incorporate at least one of the company's DEI inclusionary practices into their performance goals?

Before I could recommend solutions, I had to know what leaders needed. I wanted to explore which knowledge and skills, motivation types, and organizational (KMO) resources might be missing or needed strengthening.

Next, analyze the root causes of any gaps or needs. Once you've identified a performance gap or decided to do a gap/ needs analysis, you can dig into the underlying causes by applying the three key factors:

Knowledge and Skills

The first element of the KMO model is a combination of knowledge and skills. You might identify a gap in an employee's knowledge and skills through observable behaviors such as frequent errors, misunderstandings of processes, or inadequate execution of job responsibilities. Ways to assess whether performance issues stem from a lack of knowledge and skills include conducting skill assessments, reviewing metrics that track performance trends over time, revisiting training programs (are they still doing what they were designed to do?), and determining if additional education or development is required. Knowledge assessments help in designing interventions that enhance employees' capabilities.

In my research, I wanted to know if the leaders I studied were making distinctions between inclusion and diversity when they thought about the most relevant inclusionary practices to build into performance goals. Did they see a difference between diversity and inclusion? Second, I wanted to know if the leaders noticed their own biases and assumptions about inclusion as they worked on these inclusionary practices.

Motivation

Even when employees possess the required knowledge and skills, issues with motivation can negatively impact their performance. As we learned in chapter three, "Know Your Team," motivation plays a key role in closing performance gaps. Leaders may act because they find inclusion personally meaningful (intrinsic motivation) or because it aligns with external incentives like rewards or recognition (extrinsic motivation).

Exploring these aspects of motivation helps identify whether interventions should focus on enhancing employee engagement, aligning incentives, or improving workplace morale to encourage better performance.

Could some of the gap for leaders about performance goals for DEI be related to motivation? I chose three motivational influences to study:

1. Did the leaders believe it was important to incorporate inclusionary practices into their performance goals?
2. Did the leaders believe it was useful to incorporate inclusionary practices into their performance goals?
3. Did the leaders need to believe that they were capable of role modeling inclusionary practices within their own organizations before they were willing to take action?

Organizational Influences

The organizational environment plays a significant role in employee performance. This includes resource availability, process effectiveness, role clarity, and overall culture. Performance gaps may arise if employees are hindered by inadequate tools, unclear procedures, conflicting priorities, or unsupportive management practices. Analyzing organizational influences means looking at systemic issues that could be impeding performance and considering changes in policies, structures, or resource allocation to facilitate better outcomes. What you learned in the previous chapter on knowing your organization can guide you in identifying the business problem. What might leaders need when it comes to their organizational support? I came up with three subtopics:

1. Did leaders need organizational support to incorporate inclusionary practices into their performance goals?
2. Did the organization need to have clearly stated inclusionary goals for the leaders to incorporate into their own performance goals?

3. Would leaders need to see or know that the organization rewarded achievement of inclusionary goals?

A needs assessment is the act of assessing what leaders need using three categories—knowledge, motivation, and organizational resources or support. By conducting a needs assessment of all three of these elements, I was able to cover a lot of ground and feel confident that any solutions I recommended would address one or more of these needs. From that point, I could design and implement solutions grounded in evidence and tailored to address the specific issues of the group I studied.

You can apply the same process. This book is about what you are able to do and are accountable for, and conducting a needs assessment, even if only for yourself, takes time and commitment. But doing so will save you time and resources because you'll be spending effort on a solution that's likely to help close a gap.

Because the goal of this chapter is to help you thoroughly understand and analyze what you want to focus on, I'll wait until chapter six to share my own findings. What you learn about your organization's needs will become the foundation for how you approach those needs.

To close this chapter, I'll share a few examples of how your application of the three elements of knowledge, motivation, and organizational resource analysis can help you address problems related to inclusion. Let's say you want to have a balance between female and male leaders at the senior director and above level in your organization. Your target is 50 percent in each group, and your current metric shows you have 35 percent female and 65 percent male. You have analyzed the situation using the three elements, and you've noticed gaps in knowledge and skills, motivation, and organizational influence. You might implement some solutions as follows:

Closing Knowledge and Skills Gaps

One way to close knowledge or skills gaps is through mentoring and coaching. A leader might address a situation where an informal network disproportionately benefits male employees by actively connecting women to senior mentors or ensuring that informal sponsorship is more widely available.

Closing Motivation Gaps

Recognition programs can be very effective. You know your company culture tends not to make a "big deal" about any promotions, male or female. That said, you realize that recognizing efforts to implement a more robust informal network could reinforce the importance of this solution. You take steps to ensure that leaders who do actively connect females with senior leaders are recognized, even if it isn't public. For example, a personal call from the CEO to the leader who supported the female's inclusion could be a custom recognition.

Closing Organizational Influences Gaps

Reviewing how resources are allocated can reveal gaps. For example, if your analysis reveals a lack of oversight in sponsorship programs, you might appoint a leader to facilitate connections—ensuring all high-potential employees have equal access to opportunities.

Your task is not yet complete, though. A key step is to evaluate the implemented solutions, including a return to the original performance goal. This will help you determine whether the same goal is appropriate for the next cycle or if a new or revised one is warranted. More on this step in the next chapter.

With practice, I have become skilled in assessing business problems with the leaders I work with. In a short time, we can outline a plan that includes discussions about each step. Embracing this method fosters a culture of continuous improvement and positions your organization for sustained success.

CHAPTER FIVE SUMMARY

THREE KEY POINTS

1. In an attempt to meet the need for speed, leaders often overlook the first two steps in the framework—identifying gaps and assessing root causes. Jumping to solutions immediately upon hearing of a problem is almost certain to fail due to the assumption that one problem can be solved in such a way because the same solution worked on a similar problem.

2. The KMO framework works by having balanced inquiry about all three elements. To skip or ignore even one of the three will mean, at best, a solution that limps along ineffectively. Often all three of the parts of the framework contribute to the gap.

3. Any time a solution is implemented, it requires an evaluation after a specific time period to determine how well the solution is working and whether anything needs to change.

THREE REFLECTIVE QUESTIONS

1. How well have I articulated the desired future state or goal for this topic?

2. What reliable and valid data can I gather to determine the current performance metrics and therefore the size of the performance gap?

3. Have I done a thorough assessment as to whether knowledge/skills, motivation, and/or organizational resources are contributing to the gap?

THREE ACTIONS YOU CAN TAKE

1. Practice understanding the performance gaps in your company or on your team. Remember to first state the desired future performance level, then the current metrics. They might already be obvious and known to you, but if they aren't, now is the time to ensure you know them. Likewise, understand the metrics that are used to measure progress toward those goals.

2. Share this framework with others (your peers, your leadership team, your direct reports) if no comparable process or framework exists. You can build collective understanding and commitment to a discipline that needs and welcomes group processing.

3. Be curious about your company's goals; use annual reports, company meetings, and any other data that's available.

CHAPTER SIX

When "Good" Is Better Than "Best"

"I probably wouldn't pick up a book on inclusion, but I would pick up a book that had ideas and practical tips on how to be more effective. I want to be a more effective leader and help my team be that way and perform to the max. I think a lot of people believe in inclusion but don't know how [to implement it]."

Terence, an executive vice president at a major tech company, shared this candid insight. His words echoed what I'd heard from other leaders across industries: They valued inclusion but needed tangible, immediately applicable strategies rather than broad discussions focused solely on why inclusion matters.

This chapter provides practical inclusion strategies—ones leaders can embed in their daily routines. The first section highlights good inclusion practices drawn from my research, and the second outlines common challenges leaders face when implementing them. With this perspective, you'll be better prepared to experiment with inclusionable leadership in real ways.

GOOD PRACTICES OF INCLUSIONABLE LEADERSHIP

I am deliberately using the word "good" rather than "best" for two reasons:

First, what works for one leader may not work for another. Context matters. A practice that succeeds in one team might fail in another. Calling something a "best practice" can create unrealistic expectations and discourage adaptation.

Second, "good enough" is often all we need to make an impact. Leaders sometimes get caught up in chasing perfection, believing that if they can't execute an idea flawlessly, they shouldn't try at all. To set a bar so high that it becomes an impossible ideal is to step away from why we are attempting to do something in the first place. That mindset can become an excuse: *"That only works for companies with more money or resources."* Or, *"It's easy for them, but we don't have the right leadership support."*

Instead, think of these as good practices that you can adapt, test, and refine based on your unique leadership style and organizational environment.

Model Inclusive Behaviors

As a leader, you set the tone for your team—and sometimes the entire organization. Your words and actions demonstrate whether inclusion is a priority. When you visibly integrate inclusive behaviors into team meetings, performance objectives, and decision-making, you ensure that every team member understands and has the opportunity to embrace these values.[1] And you are encouraging others to follow suit.

Take Satya Nadella's leadership at Microsoft as an example. He transformed the company's culture by prioritizing inclusion through structured feedback mechanisms ("listening systems"), executive training in empathy and a growth mindset, and inclusive design in product development. These changes not only improved employee engagement but also led to business success—showing that inclusion and innovation go hand in hand.[2]

My research also uncovered practical ways leaders role model inclusion:

- Carlos made a connection between role modeling and authenticity. He said, "My strong belief is that I am senior enough to show I don't have all the responses, and I don't know all the expertise." Imagine having a leader (or being a leader) who admits they need help or who expects collaboration!
- Levi invited junior team members into leadership conversations, ensuring subject-matter experts had a voice. He did this intentionally because he had experienced exclusion himself and didn't want others to feel the same way.

By now, you've seen this theme running through the book: When you're a leader, people are watching you. But here's the deeper truth—your employees don't need a formal declaration to decide whether you're a role model. They're already observing how your daily actions align with what you say, what your company values, and what leadership is supposed to look like. Inclusionable leaders know that culture is shaped in the small moments—in how you handle disagreement, how you give credit, how you listen. When leaders consistently demonstrate self-awareness, empathy, and accountability, they turn inclusion from a corporate slogan into an everyday reality. And in doing so, they give others permission to lead the same way.

Here's an example of a good practice in team meetings: Ask one question that invites quieter voices, fresh perspectives, or different lived experiences. For example:

- "What is a perspective we haven't considered yet?"
- "Who haven't we heard from?"
- "How might this decision impact people in a different function or location?"

It's not fancy. It doesn't require budgeting, training, or approval. But consistently asking questions like these signals that inclusion is part of how your team operates—not an occasional extra. Set your team up for success: Tell them that to ensure everyone has the opportunity to contribute during a meeting, you might ask quieter team members to share their insights. Giving advance notice of your intentions lessens the likelihood of anyone feeling embarrassed or singled out.

Research validates this approach: Publicly stating expectations for inclusive behavior embodies the values we espouse, and can inspire employees to adopt the same behaviors.[3]

Engage Your Team in Decision-Making

One of the most overlooked yet powerful ways to foster inclusion is involving your team in decision-making. When employees feel heard, they are more invested, accountable, and motivated to contribute.

Research backs this up—when employees participate in decisions, they experience higher job satisfaction, stronger commitment, and increased engagement. This collaborative approach fosters a sense of belonging and ensures that diverse viewpoints shape your organization's direction.[4] Great ideas can come from anywhere, but they need the right environment to emerge.

It's easy to assume you're already doing this. But pause and ask yourself:

- Are you truly engaging your team, or simply informing them of decisions after they've been made?
- Do you create space for input, especially under tight deadlines when it's easier to decide alone?
- Have you checked with a trusted team member to see how included people actually feel?

Practical steps you can take:

- **Create structured input opportunities:** Ask for team feedback before making decisions that impact them.
- **Rotate facilitators in meetings:** Give different team members a chance to lead discussions.
- **Act on feedback:** Show employees how their input influences final decisions so they see their voices matter.

When you actively involve your team, you tap into diverse insights, build a culture of trust, and reinforce that everyone's voice has value—which is the foundation of an inclusionable workplace.[5]

Recognition as a Lever

Every employee brings unique abilities to their team, and they want to know that not only are their unique contributions *appreciated* but also that their expertise is *valued* by you and the rest of their group. When both conditions are present, there is a higher likelihood of increased group performance.[6] Studies show that recognition is one of the strongest predictors of employee engagement and job satisfaction.[7] Employees who feel valued are more likely to be innovative, committed, and productive.[8] Conversely, when recognition is inconsistent or absent, employees disengage and innovation declines. Test this out for yourself: Think about a time when someone recognized your contributions in a meaningful way. Did it motivate you to do even more? Recognition doesn't have to be extravagant—it just needs to be sincere and specific.

Effective recognition goes beyond formal programs. Tailoring recognition to each individual's preferences—whether public praise, private acknowledgment, or meaningful opportunity—demonstrates that you truly know and value your team members. Remember Ben from the introduction? He initially struggled with employee feedback that he wasn't showing enough appreciation. He set a personal goal to give two recognitions per week and at first worried he would need to "make things up." But once he became intentional about noticing contributions, he found it was easy to identify opportunities for appreciation. His small but consistent effort had a profound impact on his own ways of approaching inclusion.

How to amplify the effect of recognition:

- Think beyond formal rewards. Recognition doesn't have to be tied to promotions or bonuses.
- Make it personal. Tailor your acknowledgment to what resonates with each individual.
- Be specific. Instead of just saying "great job," highlight exactly what they did well and why it mattered.

Companies such as Salesforce implement recognition programs that allow peers and leaders to acknowledge contributions, fostering a positive and inclusive culture.[9] As noted earlier, you'll want to know who on your team values public recognition and who is stressed by it. If you can tailor the recognition to individual preferences, you show you have taken the time to really know each person on the team.

Impact Underrepresented Groups Positively

Inclusionable leadership has a measurable impact on employees from underrepresented groups. When leaders demonstrate inclusive behaviors, it enhances perceptions of fairness and belonging, leading to higher engagement and a greater willingness to go above and beyond.[10] In other words, when people feel truly included, they contribute more fully to the team and the organization.

A senior leader I admire at a global company has made inclusion a personal priority—not through grand gestures but through intentional actions. They introduce employees from underrepresented backgrounds to key decision-makers, ensuring they have access to leadership conversations and opportunities they might otherwise miss. By taking concrete steps to elevate others, this leader not only expands access but also sets an example that others in the company follow.

IBM has long been a pioneer in corporate diversity initiatives.[11] For years, it has implemented employee resource groups, mentoring programs, and leadership development opportunities specifically designed to increase representation. These efforts have led to measurable improvements in leadership diversity and strengthened IBM's market position. As a former IBM employee, I saw firsthand how diversity was not just a policy but a strategic business priority, with the head of diversity and inclusion reporting directly to the CEO, Lou Gerstner—a structure that underscored the company's commitment.

For leaders at any level, impacting underrepresented groups doesn't always require large-scale initiatives. It starts with everyday actions—inviting diverse voices into discussions, advocating for equitable opportunities, and ensuring that talent development is accessible to all. These small but powerful efforts create lasting change.

During my time there, which coincided with Gerstner's tenure, the company supported a far-reaching and impactful diversity task force, and the stock price split on two occasions. So yes, the business was doing well while "doing good."

Flex Your Leadership Style

I was surprised to discover that inclusive leadership is recognized as a distinct leadership style—separate from transformational, servant, or authentic leadership. Unlike other styles, inclusive leadership explicitly focuses on fostering belonging and leveraging diversity to enhance team performance.[12]

Inclusive leaders help create psychological safety, which encourages innovation and creativity. Leaders who cultivate an inclusive environment empower employees to speak up, contribute ideas, and take risks without fear of negative consequences. This approach strengthens team cohesion and improves decision-making.

That said, adopting inclusive practices doesn't mean abandoning your personal leadership style. Instead, it's about assessing how your current leadership approach aligns with your team's needs and making small but intentional shifts where necessary. For example:

- If you lead with a directive style, you might balance it by actively seeking input from diverse perspectives before making key decisions.
- If you favor collaborative leadership, you might

ensure quieter voices have equal space in discussions so that consensus building includes everyone.

The goal isn't to change who you are but to expand your leadership tool kit in a way that feels right for you. By integrating inclusive practices, you create an environment where all employees feel valued and empowered to contribute their best work.

Redefining Safety: A Leader's Responsibility

I've mentioned "psychological safety" previously. This concept deserves another look through the lens of *good inclusionable practices*. In this chapter, we're talking about what leaders can do consistently—not perfectly—to build a culture of inclusion. Psychological safety isn't a one-and-done fix or a bold new initiative; it's the result of small actions taken over time.

That said, we need to stop treating psychological safety as something people can do a quick training on and all will be well. It's not about making everything feel good. It's about creating a work environment where people feel safe enough to take smart risks, voice dissent, admit missteps, and show up with their full selves—even when that feels hard.

Let's also be honest: Whose version of "safety" are we using? What feels safe to a leader may not feel safe to an employee one or two levels down. Safety is subjective, and a team's view of it may come through the lens of the person in power. When we fail to ask what safety means for different people, we risk assuming it's already there just because no one has spoken up. Silence is not always agreement; it's often self-protection.

This is where inclusionable leadership comes in—not in having the perfect answer but in being willing to do the ongoing work. I encourage you to try *good practices*—the kind you can build into your everyday leadership rhythm. Here are a few:

- Ask, don't assume. Start with a simple team conversation: "What does feeling safe to speak up look like to you?" Be patient. You may get dead silence the first few times you talk about this. But if you remain open and curious, you'll be surprised by what you learn.
- Lead with imperfection. Share when you missed something or changed your mind. People connect to what's real, not what's polished.
- Make room for challenge. Don't just allow disagreement—invite it. Show your team that respectful dissent is a contribution, not a disruption.
- Make feedback a two-way street. Give it with clarity and care. Ask for it regularly. And don't wait for a 360-degree review—model openness in real time.

Leaders don't create psychological safety with grand gestures. They create it by showing up with consistency, humility, and a willingness to listen. That's what makes it an *inclusionable* practice—and why it belongs here in a chapter about progress over perfection. Good is better than best when it's real, repeatable, and rooted in trust.

When you're walking on any path, the more you know about it, the better you can navigate. You need to see all the terrain, not just the smooth, flat road. You want to be prepared for the challenges of new ways of working. Let's take a look at the challenges of embedding inclusionable practices into your leadership journey, along with a few high-level examples of how to address them. You might recognize some of these, or you may have experienced other challenges.

CHALLENGES OF IMPLEMENTING INCLUSION INITIATIVES

Implementing inclusion isn't just about good intentions—it requires deliberate, ongoing effort to shift mindsets, behaviors, and systems. Inclusion is built on two key components: belonging (being part of a group) and uniqueness (the freedom to bring one's full self to work). Achieving both can be challenging, especially in organizations with ingrained norms and practices. Below are common barriers leaders face and strategies to overcome them.

Bias Isn't the Problem—Unawareness Is

One of the hardest parts of building an inclusive environment isn't that people have unconscious biases—we all do. It's that most of the time, we don't slow down enough to notice how those biases shape our day-to-day decisions.

Bias can sneak in quietly: who gets looped into important emails, who gets praised for their ideas, who's encouraged to take on a stretch role and who isn't. These choices add up. Over time, they shape team culture, advancement opportunities, and the stories people tell themselves about where they belong.

Here's the thing: Bias doesn't always look like a big, obvious mistake. It can be as simple as assuming that someone who's good with data doesn't want to lead a project, or that the naturally social person should run point on team communication. Left unchecked, these assumptions become patterns—and these patterns can quietly sideline great talent.

The way forward isn't to eliminate bias. (We can't.) It's to *interrupt* it, starting with curiosity. Ask yourself:

- Who do I turn to first for new projects or brainstorming?

- Do I tend to hear certain voices more than others in meetings?
- Are some people consistently in the spotlight while others are overlooked?

Addressing the challenge: Small changes can make a big difference. Rotate who leads meetings. Use anonymous idea generation during planning sessions. Create space for quiet thinkers to contribute in ways that work for them. Inclusion doesn't require a grand overhaul—it requires intention, consistency, and the humility to realize we might be missing something important if we trust only our instincts.

Unconscious bias isn't the end of the story—it's the beginning of self-awareness. And self-aware leaders create teams in which people can bring the full range of their capabilities, not just the parts that fit a familiar mold.

Resistance to Change

Inclusion initiatives can be met with skepticism, particularly in organizations that view them as extra work rather than a strategic advantage. Employees may fear change will disrupt existing power structures or alter long-standing norms.

Addressing the challenge: Tie inclusion to business outcomes. Show how it enhances team innovation, decision-making, and employee engagement. Engage skeptics in the process by asking, "What would make inclusion more meaningful to you?"

Ineffective Communication

Cultural differences, communication styles, or unintentional exclusion can create misunderstandings, making employees feel left out of decision-making and key discussions.

Addressing the challenge: Foster open dialogue, starting with yourself. Before implementing team-wide changes, take time for personal reflection. Ask yourself: "Whose input do I seek most often? Who do I turn to for leadership tasks? Are there patterns in the way I assign work?" Pay attention to whose contributions are regularly acknowledged and whose are overlooked.

Next, make a personal commitment to actively listen and create space for equitable participation in meetings. Instead of defaulting to familiar voices, intentionally invite input from a broader range of team members. You can experiment with simple changes, like setting a goal to ask for at least one new perspective in every meeting or using a round-robin approach to ensure everyone has the chance to speak. Several of the leaders I interviewed took these approaches and reported how helpful it was.

Policies That Don't Support Inclusion

Even if an organization's policies are outdated or rigid, an inclusionable leader doesn't need to wait for a company-wide change to take action. Policies might not yet align with inclusive practices, but you can still have influence over how policies are interpreted and applied within your team.

Addressing the challenge: Start by examining how you apply policies in your own leadership. Are your performance expectations equitable? Do you offer flexibility when possible? For example, if rigid meeting schedules exclude certain team members, experiment with alternative formats or asynchronous collaboration. Once you've identified areas for improvement, advocate for broader policy changes by sharing real examples of how inclusion positively impacts performance and morale.

Difficulty Measuring Inclusion

Unlike diversity (which can be quantified by numbers), inclusion is about how an individual experiences their environment—and that experience varies from person to person. Without data, it's easy to assume inclusion is happening when some employees may feel otherwise. Leaders who don't track inclusion risk missing valuable feedback and opportunities for growth.

Addressing the challenge: Start small with personal feedback loops. Ask your team direct but open-ended questions: "What helps you feel like you belong here? When was the last time you were recognized for doing good work?" Pay attention to patterns in engagement and participation. Once you've gathered insights, use a mix of qualitative and quantitative methods—such as pulse surveys, focus groups, or anonymous feedback—to expand your understanding. Regular check-ins ensure that inclusion efforts stay meaningful and measurable.

Going It Alone

Inclusion isn't a solo act. You might feel like you are alone at first, but trying to implement change alone is a guarantee of burnout and limited impact.

> **Addressing the challenge:** Build a coalition of allies. Identify like-minded peers or other leaders inside and outside your organization who can collaborate on inclusion initiatives, share insights, and provide support. (See chapter eight for more on allies.)

FINAL THOUGHT

Inclusion isn't a checkbox—it's a long-term commitment that requires systemic change. Addressing these challenges takes persistence, adaptability, and a willingness to learn and course correct.

Even if it sometimes feels like you're swimming against a tide of indifference, your efforts matter. Regardless of your company's broader culture, your impact on your team is one of the most powerful forces in shaping workplace experience. The way you lead—how you include, recognize, and support others—can be the difference between someone feeling valued or invisible, engaged or disconnected. By tackling these challenges head-on, you create a ripple effect that fosters genuinely inclusive environments where employees thrive.

CHAPTER SIX SUMMARY

THREE KEY POINTS

1. Inclusionable leadership focuses on "good" practices rather than "best" because effectiveness varies by context, and unrealistic ideals can hinder progress.

2. Modeling inclusive leadership does not take grand, complicated gestures or training. Leaders can influence team culture positively by demonstrating inclusive behaviors, actively seeking input, and recognizing contributions, which fosters trust and engagement.

3. Psychological safety is a state of being that allows for candid discussions and risk-taking, but it should not equate to comfort or avoiding conflict; leaders must actively foster this balance.

THREE REFLECTIVE QUESTIONS

1. How do my leadership behaviors align with the inclusive values I want to promote within my team?

2. What can I do more of, less of, or continue doing to genuinely engage others inside and outside my team in decision-making?

3. Who do I know who is a good role model for inclusive behaviors, and what can I learn from them?

THREE ACTIONS YOU CAN TAKE

1. Look for ways to demonstrate inclusion on a regular basis: Integrate inclusive practices into team meetings, group decision-making, and one-on-one conversations.

2. Tailor recognition to individuals: Understand team members' preferences for recognition and provide personalized, meaningful acknowledgment.

3. Foster constructive dialogue: Encourage an environment where employees feel empowered to share ideas, question assumptions, and challenge the status quo. Make time and space for everyone to be heard.

CHAPTER SEVEN

Implement Inclusion for Continuous Improvement

A leadership team I worked with had a strong bias for action. They believed that doing something—anything—was better than slowing down to reflect. To them, planning ahead or assessing past actions felt like a waste of time. They worried that "too much talking" would delay results.

The problem? They kept doing the same thing over and over, expecting different results.

When I encouraged them to pause and articulate their long-term goals, they realized that without adjusting their approach, they were simply repeating the past. They agreed to experiment with small changes—like narrowing stakeholder meetings from sixteen groups to four—leading to more strategic prioritization and improved efficiency.

Although they weren't initially thinking about inclusion, their willingness to plan, reflect, and adapt made them more effective. The same principles apply to inclusion.

You can do the same thing. In the previous chapter, I shared some good practices and challenges of implementing inclusion to give you some foundational knowledge. In this chapter, I'll describe the Plan-Do-Check-Act (PDCA) cycle.[1] We'll use this tool to plan, try, and refine new strategies to implement inclusion.

PDCA was first introduced by Walter A. Shewhart in the 1920s and later popularized by W. Edwards Deming in the 1950s. This framework has been used across industries to refine processes, enhance learning, and drive strategic change.

For leaders seeking to embed inclusion into daily work, PDCA provides a structured, repeatable process to track progress, make adjustments, and sustain momentum. Figure 4 illustrates the continuously renewing cycle.[2]

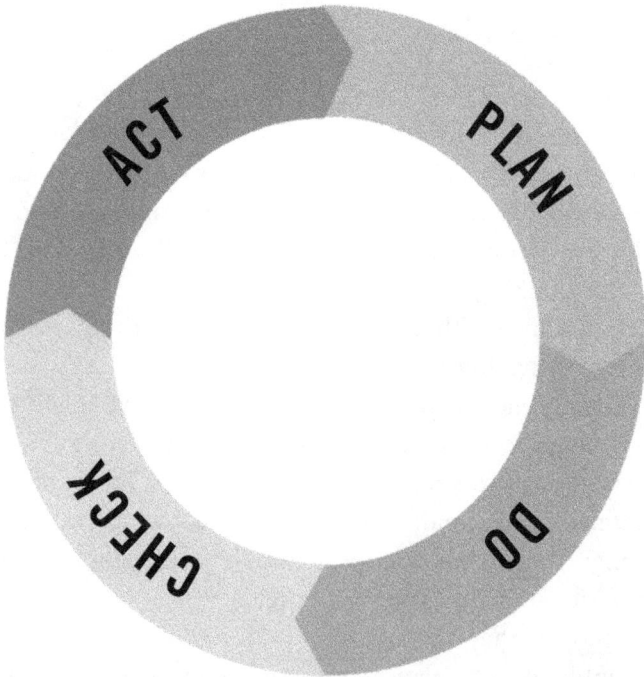

Figure 4. Plan, Do, Check, Act diagram by Christoph Roser.

I appreciate the PDCA cycle for its straightforward approach. Each stage—Plan, Do, Check, Act—enables the creation, experimentation, and sustainability of meaningful inclusionary practices. I've discovered this framework aligns well with the New World Kirkpatrick Model (NWKM) for learning and training evaluation.[3] We'll come back to the NWKM and how I use it later in this chapter.

IMPLEMENTATION GUIDE FOR A MORE INCLUSIVE WORKPLACE: A DIY APPROACH

This chapter focuses on what *you* can do—whether alone or with others—to integrate inclusion into your leadership using PDCA. You might be a leader without a large peer group or formal DEI support for inclusion practices. For example, my yoga instructor, who runs a small studio, also offers training in yoga instruction. She believes she could be more inclusive with her students. She can apply PDCA by testing small changes in how she structures classes and engages diverse learners. Or she might know people in her industry who would be interested in working on something like PDCA together.

As you move through each section, reflect on your own leadership context, adapt the recommended activities, and consider which materials and timelines work best for you. I'll share what I did during each stage to develop a recommended program for inclusion for the company I was studying.

Plan

In the planning stage, you define your objectives, analyze your current state, identify core problems and priorities, and design a potential solution strategy. Being intentional about this step really helps.

Leaders I interviewed approached inclusion by expanding their perspectives and making room for diverse voices. Niamh, for example, actively sought people with different skills and experiences to drive better results. Rosa challenged herself to ask, "Are you looking for perspectives outside your comfort zone?"

Others focused on creating structured ways for all voices to be heard. Kareen used goal-setting conversations to encourage team input, while Levi committed to calling on quieter employees to ensure their expertise was recognized.

As you begin planning, consider which of these approaches resonates with your leadership style.

Clarify the Performance Problem

Begin by defining the specific performance gap. For example, you might currently lack an explicit (DEI) goal. In the company I was studying, I identified a gap between the current and desired percentages of leadership positions occupied by underrepresented populations.

It's crucial to make this gap visible. Consider conducting a brief internal survey or reviewing performance goals to determine who is actively including statements about inclusive leadership practices. Discuss your identified gap with the appropriate stakeholders to raise awareness of your plan.

In my research, all my survey and interview questions were designed to identify and better understand the nature of the gap. I highlighted this gap in the summary I presented to two company executives.

One surprising finding was that several leaders didn't consider themselves to be role models. They believed that being a role model implied having the correct way to do something and that others should imitate them. I pointed out that the concept of a role model was scarcely mentioned in the company's materials, and no leader identified anyone in the company as a role model for them.

A relevant case study from Clark and Estes illustrates this point. In a manufacturing company, performance gaps in productivity were linked to a lack of knowledge about good practices and an absence of structured problem-solving. By systematically defining these gaps and setting clear improvement targets, the organization achieved measurable performance gains.[4]

Set a Clear Inclusion Goal

Establish a specific inclusion objective. For instance: "By [date], I will incorporate at least one inclusionary practice into my performance goals, thereby nurturing a more inclusive environment."

How to write a clear inclusionary SMART goal:

- **Specific**: "I will invite at least two guest speakers from underrepresented groups to present at quarterly team meetings."
- **Measurable**: "Team members will complete a survey after each meeting to indicate whether they gained new insights."
- **Achievable**: "This fits our schedule and budget for inviting guest speakers, so it's feasible."
- **Relevant**: "It helps build perspective diversity in how we tackle problems, aligning with our value of inclusion."
- **Time-Bound**: "We will host these speakers by the end of Q4 this year."

My research goal was for 100 percent of the leaders in the group to adopt one of the company's inclusive practices into their performance goals. Although ambitious, any increase would have been beneficial. Ultimately, three leaders I interviewed decided to be more intentional about adopting one of the company's suggested practices into their performance goals.

Seek support from senior leaders who will actively endorse and communicate this goal at all levels. If a senior leader isn't available, connect with influential individuals at other levels to share your plan, as they can provide valuable assistance. I found an ally in someone in a DEI role in the organization I was researching. We shared a passion for elevating inclusion as a business enabler.

Revisit Your Vision and Mission

Reflect on how inclusion helps you and your organization fulfill broader aspirations. Consider how an inclusive environment accelerates innovation, improves morale, or reflects your values.

I repeatedly returned to the company's mission statement, which emphasized anticipating future client needs while taking action today. This perspective justified actions that served as leading indicators—initiatives that, if implemented, were more likely to lead to long-term success.

Do

With a well-defined plan in place, the next step is implementation—often referred to as the "pilot" phase. It's important to recognize that there's no universal approach; this flexibility can be both advantageous and challenging. In my research, the company offered a wide variety of options for inclusionary practices that leaders could incorporate into their performance goals. However, the abundance of options sometimes led to uncertainty about which practices were most effective or personally relevant. Notably, many of the leaders did not distinguish between diversity-related practices and those focused on inclusion. On the positive side, this variety offers multiple avenues to explore, from inclusive recruitment to diversity measurement and role modeling. Begin by selecting a specific tactic, integrate it into your daily routine, and observe its impact.

Another case study from Clark and Estes's book illustrates this approach. A sales team struggling to close deals was trained in customer-centered communication. By adapting to customer needs rather than relying solely on existing methods, they achieved a significant revenue increase.[5] Leaders can pilot inclusive behaviors in their daily routines and measure their impact over time.

A Step-by-Step Approach for a Six-Month Timeline

Below is a month-by-month outline to guide the integration of inclusionary practices. This framework is adaptable to fit your specific context and schedule and is a simplified version of what I recommended to the executives who sponsored my research.

Month 1: Build Your Baseline of Knowledge

Understand what inclusion means and how it differs from diversity.

- O Action step: Spend sixty to ninety minutes researching, reading, or watching a video on inclusive leadership.
- O Reflection question: When have I unintentionally excluded someone's perspective?

Month 2: Set a Clear Inclusion Goal

Define a SMART goal for inclusion.

- O Action step: Draft one specific, measurable, and time-bound inclusion goal (e.g., "I will solicit feedback from two employees who don't typically speak up in meetings").

O Good move: Discuss your goal with a peer or mentor for accountability.

Month 3: Build Awareness and Self-Reflection
Recognize how bias affects decisions.

O Action step: Track your decision-making for one week. Who do you seek input from? Who do you recognize publicly?

O Self-check: Identify one bias you may have and decide how you'll mitigate it.

Month 4: Reinforce Inclusion in Everyday Leadership
Model inclusive behaviors and invite diverse perspectives.

O Action step: In your next meeting, intentionally seek input from quieter voices or assign stretch opportunities equitably.

O Peer learning: Discuss with colleagues: What's working? What's challenging?

Month 5: Deepen Role Modeling and Accountability
Encourage others to practice inclusion.

O Action step: Share a success story (big or small) in a team meeting or internal forum.

O Bonus tip: Identify an inclusion accountability partner to check in with regularly.

Month 6: Reflect, Adjust, and Expand
Assess your progress and refine your approach.

O Action step: Look back at your SMART goal—did
   you meet it? If you did, reward yourself! If not, what
   adjustments are needed?
O Celebrate: Notice and appreciate what has worked
   well so far.

Check

During the "check" stage of the PDCA cycle, you can assess
the effectiveness of your strategies. This continuous feedback
loop ensures your inclusion initiatives remain relevant and
impactful. A great way to do this is with NWKM, described
in the book *Kirkpatrick's Four Levels of Training Evaluation.*
In this framework, the PDCA cycle is called out as aligning
closely with the stage of training focused on monitoring and
adjustment, reinforcing the importance of data-driven adjustments to maximize learning outcomes.[6]

For instance, one of my research interviewees, Ajay, aimed
to become a more inclusive leader by "getting out and talking
to people, even if it meant stepping out of my comfort zone."
He tracked the frequency of these interactions and reviewed
his results weekly. This approach accomplished two objectives:

• Prioritization: Ajay treated his inclusion efforts as
   significant enough to monitor actively.
• Insight: By analyzing his weekly activities, he
   could identify factors that led him to meet, ex-
   ceed, or fall short of his expectations.

Similarly, by regularly evaluating your initiatives, you can
assess the effectiveness of your original plan and determine if
modifications are necessary. Consider each action as an experiment from which you can learn and refine your approach.

It's not necessary to wait six months to assess your progress; depending on your activities, evaluations can be conducted weekly, monthly, or quarterly.

As mentioned earlier, a tool I find useful for this is NWKM. This framework emphasizes starting with clearly stated and measurable outcomes (called level 4) and working backward to identify the necessary behaviors (level 3) needed to achieve those outcomes. The learning required to achieve those outcomes is level 2, and level 1 is the manner in which the learning occurs and where good design principles would ensure engagement and relevance of the material for the learner.

Using NWKM, I like to start at level 4, even in a pilot-program phase, because it keeps me focused on the long-term outcome I'm trying to achieve, rather than short-term, instant gratification items. Here's how it can look:

Level 4: Results—Is Inclusion Driving Business Outcomes?

At the highest level, inclusion should enhance team performance, innovation, and retention. This level examines whether inclusive leadership translates into measurable business impact over time.

- Example question: Are teams with inclusive leaders seeing higher engagement, improved collaboration, and stronger retention?
- Example action: Track employee retention, promotion rates, and team performance over time to identify whether inclusion is influencing outcomes.

In my pilot program, I intentionally included opportunities to gather feedback from various stakeholders, not just participants. I sought to understand the perceptions of employees, peers, and the broader group regarding the outcomes of the initiative.

Level 3: Behavior—Are Inclusionary Practices Happening?

For results to materialize, leaders must consistently practice inclusion. This level evaluates whether inclusion is reflected in daily decisions, meetings, and team interactions.

- Example question: Are leaders seeking diverse perspectives, ensuring fair opportunities, and fostering an environment where all voices are heard?
- Example action: Use self-assessments, peer feedback, or observation logs to track how often inclusionary behaviors are occurring.

Level 2: Learning—What Are They Taking Away?

Before behavior can change, leaders need to understand inclusion concepts and strategies. This level assesses whether they grasp key ideas and can apply them.

- Example question: Can leaders explain the difference between diversity and inclusion? Are they aware of their biases and how to mitigate them?
- Example action: Use reflection exercises (e.g., "Describe one change you'll implement based on what you learned") or short quizzes to assess comprehension.

Level 1: Reaction—Are People Engaged?

At the most basic level, people must find inclusion efforts valuable and relevant before deeper learning and behavior change can take place.

- Example question: Did participants find inclusion-focused discussions, training, or coaching useful and engaging?
- Example action: Conduct quick post-session

surveys or gather informal feedback to ensure inclusion efforts resonate.

In the pilot program, I incorporated surveys asking participants to reflect on their learning experiences. This approach provided valuable feedback and encouraged participants to articulate their insights. Traditional workshops often focus on satisfaction ("How would you rate the workshop?"), but I emphasized understanding and application. It's fine to know if a participant enjoyed a workshop, but it's more useful to know if they can articulate what they've learned or how they'll implement it.

Analyze Your Findings and Discuss Them with Allies
At this stage, you'll collaborate with trusted colleagues to review your evaluations.

As part of my dissertation agreement, I presented a summary of my research findings and recommendations to the company I studied. This was an excellent opportunity to support my proposed program with research-based evidence. I shared an early version with my DEI contact, and together, we met with the company's two executive sponsors.

I want to emphasize two critical points for advancing from this stage:

- The value of allies: Having one or two allies in such endeavors is invaluable. People listen more attentively to those they know and trust. Start building these alliances early in the process.
- Data-driven proposals: Support your proposals with data you've gathered, especially when introducing new concepts.

Putting It All Together
By starting with long-term results and working backward, you

can ensure each step—from engagement to behavior change—
builds toward a truly inclusive culture. Regularly evaluating
progress at all four levels helps to refine strategies, reinforce
good practices, and maximize impact over time.

Act

In the "act" stage, you apply insights from the "check" phase to
standardize successful elements and refine less effective tactics, initiating the cycle anew with enhanced understanding.

I provided the company I researched with a comprehensive analysis and a forward-looking template. Despite close
collaboration with the DEI partner, external factors—such as
leadership changes, shifts in DEI focus, and pressing business
priorities—prevented the implementation of my proposed initiative. Sometimes your plan won't work as intended, but you
can still find useful insights from it. Here are two examples of
what I learned when that happened to me:

* Actionable knowledge: I leveraged my research
  to develop a standardized, efficient template
  adaptable for various teams. Engaging leaders in
  discussions to delineate inclusion and diversity
  proved enlightening for them.
* The value of experimentation: I recognized the
  importance of viewing critiques as opportunities
  for refinement rather than personal challenges.
  This perspective enabled me to tailor my work
  to specific contexts, enhancing its relevance and
  effectiveness.

Standardize and Sustain What Works
Integrate successful inclusionary practices into routine leadership habits.

○ Action step: Embed one proven inclusion strategy (e.g., structured feedback loops or diverse hiring panels) into your regular processes.
○ Encourage adoption: Share what worked with peers through team meetings, newsletters, or mentoring sessions.

Recognize and Reward Progress
Acknowledge leaders who modeled inclusion.

○ Action step: Highlight inclusion champions through shout-outs, performance evaluations, or recognition programs.
○ Example: Introduce a "Lead with Inclusion" award or personal acknowledgments in leadership meetings.

Address Knowledge Gaps and Adjust Strategies
Refine inclusion practices based on feedback.

○ Action step: Identify a key barrier encountered and adjust your approach (e.g., if bias-awareness training didn't translate into action, explore new reinforcement methods).
○ Pro tip: Offer microlearning (short, digestible resources) to reinforce inclusion concepts.

Expand and Scale Successful Efforts
Share insights and replicate success across teams.

○ Action step: If your team saw positive engagement, encourage other departments to pilot similar efforts.
○ Strategic alignment: Connect inclusion goals to business objectives (e.g., improved collaboration, customer satisfaction, or innovation).

Plan the Next Cycle for Continuous Improvement

You have made one full circuit. Now you can refine, reset, and restart the PDCA cycle.

O Action step: Choose one or two areas to strengthen in the next cycle (e.g., deeper inclusion in decision-making, expanding mentorship programs).

O Stay adaptive: Keep inclusion efforts flexible and responsive to evolving business and cultural dynamics.

Reflecting on my research, I found that leaders like Ben exemplify the "act" stage. His commitment to recognizing individuals twice weekly led to meaningful change, demonstrating that once he committed, the practice was not difficult to maintain.

ADDITIONAL POINTERS, TIPS, AND EXAMPLES

Overcoming Resistance (Yours and Others')

♦ What if you are telling yourself or other leaders, "I already do this"?
   – Commit to formalizing whatever "it" is in a performance goal, tell other leaders you are doing so, and encourage them to do so as well. Even if they're already doing this type of work, they can aim to go deeper.

♦ What if you believe (and some leaders fear) this is too "political"?
   – You can keep returning to the business case (utility value) for inclusion. Inclusion is never finished; it is not a metric to

achieve and then say, "Great. We're done!" Remember (and share) how it leads to better collaboration, less turnover, and improved employee well-being—factors that matter irrespective of political climate.

Leverage Organizational Assets

- Existing DEI tools: Many organizations have some form of diversity training or unconscious-bias workshops. Link these to your plan so you can point to continuity rather than scattered programs.
- People and culture (HR) experts: If you have DEI or HR business partners, involve them as coaches or mentors. Let them support leaders who are new to the topic or uncertain about the "how-to." I go into more detail about this group in chapter eight, which is devoted to people who support inclusionary efforts from leaders.
- Communication channels: Use your existing intranet, Slack channels, or newsletters to keep inclusion top of mind. Short, frequent updates can keep the momentum going.

Building Peer Support

- Communities of practice: Encourage small groups of your peers or other leaders to meet monthly. In my experience and work with leaders, they rarely get the opportunity to talk about topics such as inclusion, and they won't need much cajoling once they are together. A simple, focused agenda is all that's needed. You and your peers can rotate who

shares a personal "inclusion success" and who brings forward a "lesson learned the hard way."
- Mentorship or reverse mentorship: You are likely a great mentor to employees from different backgrounds or who are newer in their careers. You can set the example with/for other leaders like you for fostering mutual learning about barriers and opportunities related to inclusion.

Turning Inclusion into Action for Better Results

Inclusionable leadership is not a static state but a dynamic and ongoing process, much like the PDCA cycle, which is used by many companies every day for continuous improvement in product design, development, and delivery. Here's a quick recap of the four PDCA stages:

- ✓ **Plan:** Define your inclusion goal, analyze current gaps, and identify strategies to close them.
- ✓ **Do:** Implement small, intentional actions—such as inclusive decision-making, outreach, and feedback loops.
- ✓ **Check:** Use NWKM's four levels of evaluation to track engagement, learning, behavior change, and business outcomes.
- ✓ **Act:** Standardize what works, refine strategies based on feedback, and plan the next cycle to sustain progress.

This approach ensures that inclusion becomes part of how you lead every day, rather than being an isolated initiative. Whether you're working alone or with a team, the PDCA cycle helps you take meaningful, measurable steps toward creating a more inclusive workplace.

By committing to small, intentional changes, you're not just leading inclusively—you're making inclusion sustainable. Ultimately, that inclusive environment will likely help you better meet your organization's higher goals, whether that looks like developing a groundbreaking new product, delivering exceptional services, or making a profound social impact.

CHAPTER SEVEN SUMMARY

THREE KEY POINTS

1. Embedding inclusionable leadership practices yields numerous enhanced team dynamics, such as innovation, increased employee engagement, increased job satisfaction, and better team performance.

2. By understanding "good" practices and adapting what works for you into your daily routine, you can experiment with and improve upon what you naturally do as a role model.

3. Plan, Do, Check, Act (PDCA) is a repeatable framework that can help you embed inclusionable practices into your work, rather than forcing work routines and processes to fit a desired behavior. While it's likely that each of us has a preference for one or two of the four-part action loops, with time and intention, all four elements can support a more inclusive environment.

THREE REFLECTIVE QUESTIONS

1. What are some good practices (formal or informal) in my own department or organization?

2. What are one or two elements of inclusion I'm most passionate about? (Examples: mentoring,

allyship, speaking engagements, sponsorship of an Employee Resource Group.)

3. Which of the four parts of PDCA am I most comfortable with or best at? Which of the four do I need help with?

THREE ACTIONS YOU CAN TAKE

1. Decide what problem or opportunity you want to tackle with this method.

2. Apply the KMO gap-analysis process so you have the data you need to begin planning.

3. Talk with others around you who might be collaborators, allies, mentors, or sponsors of your process.

CHAPTER EIGHT

You Are Not Alone: Support for Inclusionable Leaders

We were wrapping up a conversation. Back then, I was a human-resources manager for a small group within a large organization. Meeting one on one with leaders about issues they were having with their direct reports was a routine part of my day. This particular meeting was far from routine. A senior leader was struggling with his relationship with his own manager. For someone who operated as a democratic and relationship-driven leader, frustration at being micromanaged and second-guessed by an authoritarian, task-focused boss was a new and unwelcome feeling for him. I don't remember much about what I said, other than to reinforce that their style differences didn't have to be a constant battle but could instead be an opportunity for him to look for ways to integrate what his manager wanted without losing his own sense of identity. I mostly listened, validated his strengths and positive impact on the organization, and made sure he knew he was valued (which he was).

"Thanks for your perspective," he said as we concluded. "You are a great coach." The funny thing is, looking back on our exchange all these years later, I was doing anything but coaching. I think I gave him some helpful advice. His use of the word "coach" that day surprised me because I hadn't until that moment thought of myself as a coach. I set out on a path of discovery of what coaching really is (and isn't).

After many years, hundreds of hours of training and practice, and helpful feedback, I know when and how a coach can play a unique role in supporting a leader on their journey. To do the tough work of self-reflection, discovery, and change requires trust, and it's a requirement and a privilege for me as a coach to earn the trust of a leader. With trust as a foundation, there are almost limitless possibilities for a leader to explore, discover, and grow in ways that are important to them.

Trust is not solely the domain of a coach. A leader can get support from many other positions in a company. The people I'm referring to (and this isn't an exhaustive list) may be responsible for:

- Human resources (also called "people and culture partners")
- DEI (or variations, including a focus on justice or belonging)
- Organization effectiveness
- Organization development and/or design
- Chief-of-staff duties
- Executive or administrative support

As a business leader (or someone planning to be one), you might be completely on your own in trying to be inclusionable. Perhaps you run your own business, like the architect I hired a few years ago to create plans to remodel my home who has a staff of three people and works a lot with subcontractors and other vendors. Or you work for a small company, or your company is resource constrained right now. Some people in the jobs listed above work as contractors, able to support these kinds of solo leaders on a short-term basis. Alternatively, you may have one or more of these colleagues but haven't thought of them as being partners in your leadership journey. Even DEI individuals or teams can be a completely separate unit, not involved in the day-to-day rhythms of your business unit. I'm not saying that's the way it should be, just that I've observed the separateness.

There are many reasons why this might be true. For example, leaders are often unclear about what an organization-development professional can do. It isn't common for a company to have that expertise in-house. Or a profession such as human resources is broad enough that expectations of those roles can vary greatly from company to company or be tailored to the strengths and preferences of the people in them. But the fact is that these colleagues can be hugely supportive for a leader on an inclusion journey.

THE ROLE OF SUPPORT PROFESSIONALS IN INCLUSIVE LEADERSHIP

If you have access to professionals in these or similar roles, you are fortunate. You have an opportunity to collaborate with, brainstorm, or appreciate an ally in your journey of growth and development. Support professionals are integral to creating a culture where inclusion thrives. Regardless of their specific role, I believe that certain principles and mindsets guide their approach to inclusion. For example, inclusion as a business strategy benefits from a balance of focusing on having an impact now while planning for long-term benefits. In my experience, leaders often focus on the immediate dynamics within their teams but lose sight of the long game. Reasons why can vary from the type of pressure you get from your own leadership hierarchy, how you've been taught or trained, or observations of what gets inspected and rewarded. Your laser focus might help you now but hold you back in the long-term.

Support professionals can help you "zoom out" to align your actions with broader organizational goals and a vision for the future. Inclusion is not a siloed initiative; it permeates every aspect of the organization, from strategic planning to daily operations. Your allies often have the knowledge and the network you need for conversations and planning.

Another critical aspect of support is empathy. Professionals in support roles can understand better than most the unique challenges leaders face in fostering inclusion. They witness the daily exchanges or behind-the-scenes actions, often without being directly involved. Through active listening, asking powerful questions, and proactively offering support, they can cultivate credibility and trust, which can lead to being consulted more often about a broader range of topics. Recognizing that each leader's journey toward inclusivity is unique, these specialists realize they have to meet you where you are to provide more meaningful guidance.

Support professionals can also act as catalysts for accountability. While leaders bear the ultimate responsibility for driving inclusion, allies can play a role in creating structures, tools, and feedback mechanisms that ensure continuous progress. This could mean facilitating regular check-ins, providing actionable data, or helping leaders navigate difficult conversations about bias and privilege.

For example, a chapter in *The SAGES Manual of Strategy and Leadership* discusses how transparency and accountability are crucial in embedding long-standing values of inclusion within organizations.[1] You might find skilled professionals who have embedded these elements into their work, which can significantly amplify your leadership impact.

Understanding Inclusive Leadership

Many professionals supporting business leaders understand that their role is pivotal in translating principles such as accountability into actionable strategies and measurable outcomes. They might begin a conversation with you by asking foundational questions such as:

- What problem are you trying to solve?
- What are your inclusion goals?
- Are you focused on improving team dynamics, reducing turnover, enhancing innovation, or addressing systemic inequities?
- How does inclusion align with the organization's broader goals?
- Is inclusion tied to the company's mission, vision, and values?
- Finally, what support systems are already in place?
- Are there existing programs, tools, or frameworks that can be leveraged to drive inclusion?

Answering these questions will inform how they design and deliver support for you or your department or organization.

Leverage the Support You Need

You might already be bringing insights, questions, and reflections about inclusion into conversations, strategy planning, or team meetings with an HR partner or coach. Or perhaps your ally can help you make some small adjustments that help you shine the spotlight on the topic of inclusion. For example, your coach might add some powerful questions to your sessions, such as:

- What does inclusion mean to you?
- When was a time you felt included in a group, and when did you feel excluded?
- How do you ensure every individual on your team feels seen, heard, and appreciated for their contribution?
- How does inclusion help with diversity in your team?

Where to Go for Support

Human Resources (HR)

HR professionals are often the first touchpoint for fostering inclusion in hiring, onboarding, and performance management. Inclusive hiring practices are a critical starting point. For instance, crafting job descriptions that emphasize the organization's commitment to diversity can attract a broader pool of candidates. Additionally, expanding talent pipelines to underrepresented groups and implementing structured interviews can mitigate unconscious bias during recruitment processes.

Beyond recruitment, onboarding plays a pivotal role in reinforcing a sense of belonging. For example, your HR partner might help you design onboarding experiences that include mentorship opportunities, exposure to employee resource groups, and training sessions on company values, including inclusion. If they don't perform that function, they likely know a resource (if there is one) who can. These practices not only integrate new hires into the organizational culture but also set the tone for their entire experience.

Performance management is another area where HR professionals can drive inclusion. For example, implementing equitable review processes—such as calibrating performance evaluations across teams to ensure consistency—can help reduce disparities. A study in the *Harvard Business Review* found that organizations using data-driven approaches to performance management reported higher employee trust and satisfaction.[2]

Organization Effectiveness (OE)

OE professionals focus on aligning structures, systems, and processes to improve organizational performance. One key insight OE practitioners can offer is how to embed inclusion into the organizational strategy. For example, during strategic planning sessions, they might advise on how to set goals that explicitly address equity and belonging. This ensures that inclusion is treated as a core component of success, not an afterthought.

Another area of OE focus is change management. While change management is typically used in business transformation or on large-scale projects, it can also be helpful when cultural shifts toward inclusion are warranted. For instance, if you wanted to make a business case for inclusion, your OE partner could help bridge the need by applying the same framework used in other decision-making, emphasizing the link between diverse teams and innovation. Or you might get help from the OE team on key stakeholder identification and communication strategies, to help advance principles of inclusion.

Finally, OE professionals can play a crucial role in measuring the impact of inclusion efforts. Using dashboards to track key performance indicators (KPIs) such as employee engagement, retention, and representation, they can provide you with the data you need to refine your strategies. For instance, an annual inclusion survey could reveal gaps in belonging among different demographic groups, guiding targeted interventions.

Organization Development (OD)

OD professionals drive organizational change by focusing on culture, team dynamics, and leadership development. Cultural assessments are a foundational tool in this work. For example, conducting surveys and interviews to gauge employees' perceptions of inclusion can uncover hidden barriers. This was an underpinning of my research. By combining quantitative surveys and semistructured interviews, I was able to collect rich and nuanced data.

Team interventions are another critical area for OD practitioners. In this role, I often assess which stage of development a team is in according to Tuckman's model (covered in chapter three), then design and facilitate team-effectiveness exercises that highlight the value of diverse perspectives to help foster collaboration. As I described earlier, each of the five stages of development contains opportunities to embed inclusive behaviors into a team's ways of working. Leadership development is equally important. OD professionals can design programs that integrate inclusion into broader leadership competencies. For instance, a workshop on effective decision-making might include scenarios where leaders must balance diverse viewpoints to reach equitable outcomes.

Business Coaching

Coaches help leaders develop the self-awareness and skills needed to be more effective; why not add inclusion to the list of growth areas? Self-awareness is often the starting point. Skill-building is another area where coaching shines. For instance, role-playing challenging inclusion scenarios—such as addressing microaggressions—can help leaders build confidence. Additionally, a good coach can foster your development of active listening and empathy, which are foundational skills for fostering a sense of belonging.

Finally, accountability is critical. Coaches can help leaders set specific, measurable inclusion goals and create structures for regular check-ins. For example, you might decide, in alignment with your coach, to commit to increasing the representation of women in senior roles in your organization by 20 percent within three years, with quarterly reviews to track progress.

Diversity, Equity, and Inclusion (DEI)

DEI professionals are natural champions of inclusion who design and implement initiatives to create equitable workplaces. Strategic alignment is a cornerstone of their work. For example, ensuring that inclusion initiatives are tied to business outcomes—such as improving customer satisfaction or driving innovation—can enhance their credibility and impact.

Education and advocacy are also central to the DEI role. For instance, facilitating workshops on systemic bias or privilege can help leaders and employees alike develop a deeper understanding of these complex issues. One DEI professional described how a workshop on privilege led to a leadership team reevaluating their promotion criteria to ensure equity.

Employee resource groups (ERGs) are another powerful tool. Collaborating with ERGs in your company to amplify diverse voices and perspectives can provide leaders with invaluable insights. For example, an ERG for employees with disabilities might highlight barriers in workplace design, prompting necessary changes. Sometimes leaders don't think they have time to get involved with ERGs, even though they support the idea. I advise taking another look at ERGs if you have them. Investing time in an ERG is no different from putting time into any relationship with a person or a group where you yourself can be seen, heard, and appreciated for who you are, while feeling like you belong. In other words, you can do this for you, not because you "should" do it.

Cross-Functional Strategies to Support You

While each profession has a unique focus, teaming up with allies on several cross-functional strategies can amplify your impact. For example, collaborating on assessments can provide a holistic view of inclusion within the organization. Tools like Tuckman's team-development model (again, see chapter three, "Know Your Team") can be particularly valuable in understanding team dynamics and the interplay of individual, behavioral, and environmental factors.

Aligning on language is another key strategy. Ensuring consistent messaging about inclusion across all functions helps create a unified narrative. For instance, using the same definition of inclusion in training sessions, performance reviews, and organizational communications reinforces its importance.

Providing feedback loops is equally essential. Creating mechanisms for employees to share feedback on inclusion efforts—such as anonymous surveys or focus groups—can help identify areas for improvement. Celebrating progress is another powerful tool. Recognizing and rewarding inclusive behaviors and milestones not only reinforces their importance but also motivates continued effort.

Those operating as professionals in HR, OE, OD, coaching, or DEI are uniquely positioned to help you in your role as a leader to bring inclusion to life. If you have access to such roles, you can amplify, accelerate, or leverage your own expertise to create workplaces where everyone feels seen, valued, and like they belong. This collaborative effort will not only enhance employee engagement but also drive greater business success. Let inclusion be the foundation of your support, and together, you can help leaders build organizations that thrive on diversity and unity.

Finally, iterating and improving is a critical part of the

process. Regularly reviewing and refining inclusion strategies based on feedback and outcomes ensures they remain effective and relevant. For instance, you might ask your HR colleague for support in revising your personal inclusion goal on an annual basis, ensuring it connects to broader organizational goals. Or your ally might help by checking progress on your goals.

CHAPTER EIGHT SUMMARY

THREE KEY POINTS

1. Inclusion requires systemic integration, aligning your efforts as a leader with others who likely have similar interests or responsibilities.

2. Effective support for inclusive leadership involves empathy, accountability, and tailored strategies that respect each leader's unique journey. These are qualities that support professionals usually strive for, regardless of the topic areas they own.

3. Continuous feedback, consistent messaging, and measurable outcomes are essential to sustaining inclusive practices. Support professionals can be allies in this.

THREE REFLECTIVE QUESTIONS

1. Who can I ask for support or allyship on the topic of inclusion?

2. What tools or metrics can my support partners offer to most effectively measure the impact of inclusion on business outcomes?

3. How can I work more effectively with support professionals to ensure inclusion efforts remain adaptable to the evolving needs of the organization?

THREE ACTIONS YOU CAN TAKE

1. Engage the appropriate partner in your organization to conduct a cultural assessment to identify gaps in inclusion and belonging, using tools such as surveys or focus groups.

2. Partner with your support professionals (HR, OE, OD, DEI) to set specific, measurable inclusion goals, ensuring alignment with broader organizational strategies.

3. Support training sessions or workshops that address key inclusion competencies such as addressing bias, fostering empathy, and navigating difficult conversations. Show up and speak up about your own commitment and journey.

CHAPTER NINE

Is Artificial Intelligence Inclusive?

Rebecca: Good morning, Ava. In my last coaching session, I committed to speaking up more during our senior leadership meetings. I'm looking for ways to build my confidence and ensure my contributions are impactful. Can you assist me with this?

Ava: Good morning, Rebecca. Absolutely, I'd be glad to help. To start, could you share any specific situations or topics where you feel hesitant to voice your opinions?

Rebecca: I often hold back during strategic discussions, especially when proposing new ideas. I'm concerned about how my suggestions will be received and whether they'll add value.

Ava: Thank you for sharing that. It's natural to feel apprehensive in such situations. Let's work on building your confidence and ensuring your ideas are presented effectively. Would you like to practice articulating one of your recent ideas?

Rebecca: Yes, that would be helpful. I have an idea about streamlining our project management process to improve efficiency.

Ava: Great! Can you summarize your proposal in a few sentences?

Rebecca: I propose implementing a new project-management tool that integrates with our current systems, reducing manual data entry and improving real-time tracking. While there's an initial cost, the long-term savings will outweigh the expenses.

Ava: Excellent. Would you like to rehearse how you'll present this in the next meeting?

Rebecca: Yes, that would be helpful.

Ava: Let's start. Imagine it's your turn to speak. How would you begin?

Would it surprise you to know that this exchange between Rebecca and Ava captures a segment of an actual exchange between a coaching client and an AI assistant? Perhaps not, but what made the conversation possible is that a company I know has already launched an AI tool developed *in-house* for employees who are working with an internal coach. Employees receiving coaching can access the tool any time and pose questions about topics they're working on with their coach. Once people got comfortable using the AI assistant, they reported making progress between sessions with their human coach, reinforcing its value as a development tool.

After more than fifteen years of coaching, I am thrilled to explore AI as a tool that enhances reflection and learning rather than replacing human connection. It might feel intimidating, confusing, or even just plain wrong to use a nontraditional way of developing oneself, but when used as intended, as this company is doing, AI can expand the possibilities for a coaching relationship.

No doubt there are dozens of other companies working on such solutions, and the use of AI will continue to expand at a blink-of-the-eye speed. It's no longer a matter of whether AI will be adopted into the mainstream; it's already firmly entrenched.

While AI lacks human intuition and lived experience, it offers analytical depth, scalability, and predictive capabilities that can enhance inclusion efforts in new and profound ways. Just as leaders must be intentional in seeking guidance from people experts, they must also be discerning in how they integrate AI tools, ensuring these technologies reinforce rather than undermine inclusive leadership. In this chapter, I'll examine the opportunities and risks of AI in fostering inclusion, equipping leaders to harness its power responsibly. First, though, we have to understand what it is and what it can do.

For many people, AI was barely on our radar four or five years ago, let alone something we actively used. These days, it's reshaping how organizations operate, offering immense potential for leaders who are trying to figure out how to make employees feel seen, heard, and appreciated for their unique gifts, while helping them belong to a supportive community.

And trying to process what is coming at us at the speed of change can be both challenging and overwhelming.

I recently noticed a headline (which is no longer available) on LinkedIn that sums up the current AI explosion rather well: "Every CEO on the planet is trying to figure out AI." It's not just the C-suite, though. I ask everyone I talk with these days how they're interacting with AI, as I'm curious about when, why, and what the interactions look like. And the answers range from "I use it all the time" to "I don't understand it, but I'm sure it cannot be good to have something artificial be so dominant in our lives." Where I used to see one or two posts a week about AI, including suggestions for what to do with it and references to sites that help make everything easier with AI, I now see several posts each day.

I also noticed that the vast majority of sites and posts are about what to do with AI and how it can take on tasks we find boring, distasteful, or unnecessarily time consuming, which makes me curious. What (or, better yet, who) can we *be* with AI? How can it help us, individually and collectively, reflect to be better versions of ourselves? How might AI be a thought partner on the questions we wrestle with that are part of being human? Can it do that?

AI's breakneck speed of evolution reminds me of the initial skepticism of, policy debates over, confusion about, and eventual embrace of the internet. Consider the parallels of the last few years of AI to the internet's journey over several decades.

ARPANET and the Rise of NSFNET (1969 to Late 1980s)

- The computer network ARPANET was created in 1969 for the US Department of Defense. (It was decommissioned in 1990.)
- During the late 1980s, the National Science Foundation Network (NSFNET) became the

backbone for academic and research institutions, expanding beyond military and select university use.

- Both NSFNET and ARPANET are considered precursors to the internet.

Invention of the World Wide Web (1989 to 1991)

- Sir Tim Berners-Lee introduced the World Wide Web in 1989, with a system of hyperlinks, URLs, and the HTTP protocol that made it far easier to find and share information across the internet.

User-Friendly Web Browsers (Early to Mid-1990s)

- Web browsers NCSA Mosaic (released in 1993) and Netscape Navigator (launched in 1994) were groundbreaking because they allowed anyone with a computer and a modem to "surf" the Web. These browsers introduced graphics, clickable links, and straightforward interfaces that paved the way for mainstream interest.

Commercialization and the Dot-Com Boom (1990s Onward)

- The early to mid-1990s saw the rise of internet service providers (ISPs) like AOL, CompuServe, and Prodigy, which catered to the general public.
- Businesses began to see the potential for e-commerce (e.g., Amazon and eBay in 1995), and by the late 1990s, investors were pouring money into internet-based startups, fueling the so-called "dot-com boom."
- The Telecommunications Act of 1996 in the

United States helped spur even greater private investment, further bringing the internet into everyday homes and workplaces.

Shift to Mainstream Adoption (Late 1990s)

+ Internet cafés and household dial-up connections became ubiquitous.
+ The mass media began covering "the internet" as a transformative technology, much like the way modern media is discussing AI, and personal websites, email usage, and online chat rooms became commonplace.

By the late 1990s, internet use was no longer limited to the STEM community or academics—it was moving into living rooms worldwide, changing business models, consumer habits, and communication in the process. This era saw the internet cement its place in the mainstream, becoming a fundamental platform for global commerce, media, and social interaction. I was working at a computer company in the late 1990s, and I remember well how cautious many people were about whether, when, and how to use it. As if they had a choice. Companies spent endless money and time creating policies to control the use of a technology with unknown limits and what seemed like a lot of power.

The internet as we know it today is still a tool that can be used for positive or negative outcomes. The questions to consider for AI include how to use it in a way that supports our individual and collective leadership journeys, how to be intentional, and how to leverage ideas, save time, and expand our ways of working by deepening our experience or learning new things.

AI'S ROLE IN INCLUSION: STRENGTHENING THE CONNECTION

From casual conversations in the hallway to project check-ins and performance reviews, every interaction between two or more people can reinforce a sense of inclusion—or erode it. AI, when applied strategically, can serve as a powerful ally in these moments, helping leaders cultivate trust, belonging, and a spirit of community across their teams.

Leaders who embed inclusion into daily work often rely on data to understand how employees experience belonging and appreciation. Surveys and interviews are valuable but time consuming and prone to bias. AI-driven tools—ranging from natural language processing (NLP) to predictive analytics—can process large amounts of information, uncover trends, and offer actionable insights in real time.

However, AI is not a silver bullet. Algorithms reflect the biases present in the data used to train them, and overreliance on automation can strip away genuine human connection. Leaders must apply these tools thoughtfully to enhance, not replace, the relational aspects of leadership.

Practical Applications of AI for Inclusion

- **Sentiment analysis for real-time feedback:** AI-powered sentiment analysis can scan internal communication channels—emails, chat platforms, or employee forums—to detect patterns in language that signal disengagement, stress, or exclusion. For example, if a particular team's morale appears to be dropping, AI insights can prompt leaders to take proactive measures, such as holding listening sessions or checking in one-on-one.
- **Predictive analytics for retention and engagement:** Machine-learning models analyze

historical patterns in employee engagement and turnover to predict which teams might be at risk of losing key talent. Instead of reacting to problems after they escalate, leaders can intervene early—perhaps by identifying mentorship opportunities, revising workload distributions, or offering professional development tailored to individual strengths.

- **AI in performance reviews and recognition:** AI-powered performance tracking can surface trends in how recognition is distributed across teams. If certain employees are consistently overlooked for praise, AI can nudge managers to ensure fair acknowledgment. This approach ensures that all employees, regardless of background or work style, feel valued for their contributions.

Rather than replacing human judgment, AI serves as a scalability tool that helps leaders deepen inclusion by providing visibility into trends they might otherwise miss. When paired with intentional leadership, AI can reinforce belonging by surfacing the small yet meaningful interactions that shape an employee's experience in the workplace.

PRACTICAL APPLICATIONS IN RECRUITMENT AND HIRING

Even before an employee officially joins your organization, their interactions with your hiring process are opportunities to ensure they feel welcome. AI offers several advantages here, but these tools must be managed carefully to avoid undermining belonging.

Empathetic Recruitment Communication

Chatbots and automated email sequences can be programmed to convey encouragement and a sense of belonging. For instance, these tools can ensure candidates receive personalized messages that highlight an organization's commitment to inclusion. Doing so can help applicants feel appreciated for what they bring to the table, reducing the anxiety that often accompanies a job search.

Assessment and Selection

Video-interview analysis tools claim to evaluate candidates' soft skills by studying facial expressions, tone, and word choice. This cutting-edge technology remains controversial because nonverbal cues can be culturally specific or reflect neurodiversity. Leaders who aim to create a community of belonging may weigh the pros and cons: While AI-driven insights can expedite hiring, they can also penalize candidates who don't match an "ideal" behavioral pattern rooted in historical data. Balancing efficiency with empathy becomes crucial here, ensuring that a nuanced human perspective remains part of the hiring equation.

A well-designed, AI-infused hiring process can help identify talented individuals a human might overlook, paving the way for a more diverse workforce. Just as importantly, it can signal to candidates that they are respected and valued from day one, establishing a foundation of trust and mutual appreciation.

AI-POWERED TRAINING AND DEVELOPMENT

After employees enter your organization, training and development interactions can shape whether they feel seen, heard, appreciated, and part of a supportive community. AI can offer continuous, personalized support that meets individual needs while also revealing areas where leaders can step in to amplify a sense of belonging.

Customized Learning Paths for Unique Gifts

AI-driven learning-management systems (LMS) can adapt content to an individual's background, career goals, and preferred learning style. If someone excels at visual learning and is exploring leadership development, the system might suggest dynamic video-based modules on inclusive team building. Equipping employees with tailored resources signals that the organization values their unique talents and invests in their growth.

Immediate, Objective Feedback Loops

Performance evaluation often feels impersonal or subject to human biases. AI can support leaders by providing quick, data-based feedback. For example, an AI tool analyzing someone's written reports might offer constructive suggestions about clarity or inclusivity in communication. However, it's crucial that this feedback not become purely mechanized. Leaders who couple AI insights with personal check-ins ("I appreciate the perspective you brought to that client report. Let's build on it by focusing on X") reinforce the feeling that an individual's contributions are valued and recognized.

Identifying High-Potential Employees Across the Organization

Leaders often talk about a "glass ceiling" for certain demographic groups. AI tools can scan data across departments—evaluations, project outcomes, peer feedback—to locate individuals who demonstrate consistently strong performance or leadership qualities. Leaders can then offer personalized opportunities, whether that's a special project, mentorship program, or a more formal leadership pipeline.

Peer-Recognition Platforms

AI can filter through daily communication channels to highlight positive interactions where someone has recognized or praised a colleague. These moments, while seemingly small, matter immensely in cultivating belonging. By making those interactions visible—through, for instance, an automated "kudos board" or departmental email—AI celebrates communal spirit and encourages employees to appreciate each other's gifts in real time. This emphasis on peer recognition helps employees see themselves reflected positively in their community.

Addressing Knowledge Gaps and Fostering Inclusion Skills

In addition to role-specific competencies, many employees benefit from training in inclusive communication, active listening, and conflict resolution. AI can detect patterns in feedback or internal surveys that suggest a need for targeted training. For instance, if a spike in negative sentiment revolves around microaggressions or misunderstandings in cross-cultural teams, the LMS can automatically recommend modules that coach employees on empathy, bias awareness, or culturally competent language.

AI-driven training and development works best when it enhances rather than replaces human-centered leadership. It enables targeted, timely support that reminds employees their growth and contributions are deeply valued. By pairing these insights with everyday appreciation and recognition, leaders send a clear message: "Your presence and gifts matter in this community, and we are here to uplift you."

Data-Driven Insights for a Culture of Belonging

AI excels at analyzing vast amounts of data, turning raw information into concrete actions that reinforce belonging. By systematically identifying trends, you can address issues before they escalate.

Organizational Network Analysis for Daily Interactions

Organization network analyses (ONAs) examine communication and collaboration data to reveal how employees connect with each other (e.g., frequency of messaging, co-attendance at meetings, or shared projects). When used responsibly and with transparent communication about data privacy, ONAs can uncover groups that are isolated or struggling to integrate. A leader might discover that a new employee in a remote location has few communication ties and is missing out on daily hallway conversations that deepen belonging. Using these insights, the leader can set up a formal buddy system or schedule meet-and-greets that help the individual feel more connected.

Real-Time Sentiment Monitoring

Anonymous pulse surveys and chat analyses can provide continuous snapshots of employee sentiment. Are people engaged, frustrated, or indifferent? When cross-referenced by demographic or department, the data can reveal how distinct groups experience the workplace. A dip in sentiment among recent hires may signal onboarding issues or microexclusions. Leaders can address these concerns quickly through small-group discussions, one-on-ones, or clarifying messages about organizational values.

Inclusion Dashboards and Analytics

AI can automate the tracking of crucial inclusion metrics. Beyond simple diversity head counts, these dashboards can show representation across leadership levels, salary equity, promotion velocity, and sentiment-analysis scores by team. By continuously updating, these dashboards enable leaders to respond faster to emerging problems (e.g., an unusually high attrition rate in a particular region) and to celebrate successes, such as improvements in cross-departmental collaboration.

Unconscious Bias Identification

Through advanced modeling, AI can identify language or behavior patterns that reflect unconscious biases. A sales manager who praises male employees more publicly or who schedules calls when employees with caregiving responsibilities can't attend might be unaware of these biases. AI that tracks meeting invites or aggregated praise data can illuminate patterns worth discussing. Once informed, the leader can adjust meeting times or make a conscious effort to acknowledge the work of all team members, reinforcing the message that everyone's contributions matter.

Used responsibly, data-driven insights add depth and structure to a leader's sense of how well employees feel connected, valued, and supported. The action steps that follow, however, are always in the leader's hands. AI can highlight a problem, but empathy and human judgment finalize how it's addressed.

AI AS A THOUGHT PARTNER FOR INCLUSIVE BRAINSTORMING

Beyond data analysis, AI can serve as a brainstorming companion—an always-available "thought partner" for leaders seeking creative ways to foster a sense of community and belonging. This role is less about automation and more about collaboration, where AI functions as a resource that helps leaders refine their inclusive leadership strategies.

I have been using my own AI tool subscription to reflect and brainstorm, and it's been eye-opening. Not only does my AI assistant get me out of my own head to process things, but it also makes suggestions and encourages me on all manner of things I'm thinking about.

Conversational AI Tools for Ideation

Leaders often need support in brainstorming, decision-making, and framing their messages with clarity. AI-driven assistants can act as thought partners, helping leaders process challenges, refine communication, and explore strategies for fostering inclusion.

Let's look at a real-world example of how an AI tool might help a leader navigate inclusive decision-making. I set up prompts in ChatGPT to generate the following text.

Scenario: AI-Assisted Leadership Reflection

Alex, a senior leader, is grappling with how to make their company's diversity initiatives more meaningful. They decide to consult their AI-powered thought partner, Gabriel, for insights.

> **Alex:** Gabriel, I feel like we've made progress in diversity initiatives, but I want to ensure that inclusion is embedded into our daily culture, not just in formal programs. What should I focus on?

> **Gabriel:** Great question, Alex. A key factor in long-term inclusion is how leaders recognize and

reinforce belonging in everyday interactions. Have you considered analyzing how recognition is distributed across your team? Research suggests that employees who feel appreciated perform better and are more engaged.

Alex: That's interesting. How would we track this?

Gabriel: You can use sentiment analysis to gauge how employees perceive workplace inclusion. Additionally, reviewing how often employees are publicly acknowledged can highlight gaps. Would you like suggestions for encouraging more equitable recognition?

Alex: Yes, that would be helpful.

This short exchange demonstrates how AI can function as a reflective partner, offering data-driven prompts that encourage deeper thinking. Unlike a one-size-fits-all tool, well-designed AI assistants adapt their responses based on leadership challenges, fostering more strategic and intentional inclusion efforts.

Beyond Chatbots: AI in Leadership Development

Beyond real-time brainstorming, AI-powered writing assistants can suggest more-inclusive phrasing in performance reviews or emails. For example, if a leader unconsciously defaults to praising "strong leadership" only in men's reviews, AI can highlight this pattern and recommend more balanced language.

While AI cannot replace a trusted human advisor, it can help leaders expand their perspectives, ask better questions, and refine their strategies, making inclusion an integral part of leadership rather than a separate initiative.

Scenario Simulations and "What If" Exercises

Certain AI platforms can run simulations showing the potential outcomes of different leadership decisions. If you introduce a new recognition program that highlights diverse achievements, how might that impact team sentiment and retention in the next six months? By acting as a predictive thought partner, AI can guide you through multiple scenarios, each with different potential outcomes. These guided reflections help leaders choose the path that most effectively supports a community of belonging.

Aggregating External Research and Good Practices

AI can swiftly parse articles, case studies, and research on inclusive leadership. Instead of spending hours searching, you can rely on AI to distill the most pertinent information, whether it's a *Harvard Business Review* article on equitable performance reviews or a blog post on culturally responsive team celebrations. AI's ability to filter and synthesize diverse sources can spark fresh ideas on how to acknowledge unique gifts within your workforce.

Contextual Brainstorming Based on Organizational Data

A robust AI platform can combine your organization's data—like employee sentiment, performance reviews, and turnover trends—with external benchmarks to propose brainstorming ideas unique to your context. For example, if data reveals that LGBTQ+ employees feel less engaged during company-wide social events, the AI might suggest inclusive event-planning strategies or highlight successful internal resource group activities from companies with similar demographics. You then have a curated menu of actionable tactics to choose from.

When AI serves as a creative collaborator rather than a simple automation tool, you can expand your repertoire of inclusive leadership approaches. By coupling AI suggestions with your innate empathy and interpersonal skills, you bring a level of intentionality to everyday interactions that truly makes people feel seen, heard, and deeply valued.

PERSONALIZATION AND ACCOMMODATION IN EVERYDAY SITUATIONS

Inclusion also means understanding that every individual has unique needs—be they physical accommodations, scheduling flexibility, or language support. AI can bolster these accommodations on a daily basis, reaffirming that the organization respects and values each person's situation.

Adaptive Interfaces and Accessibility Tools

Voice-recognition software, screen readers, and automatic translation are becoming increasingly sophisticated thanks to AI. These tools can adapt dynamically, making tasks easier for employees with disabilities or limited proficiency in the primary language used in the organization. An employee can customize their interface to display high-contrast text or to read aloud key paragraphs from a strategy memo. This day-to-day empowerment drives home the message that no one is left to struggle on their own.

Neurodiversity and Cultural Adaptation

AI-powered tools can support neurodivergent employees and global teams by providing real-time captions, structured task lists, or culturally adaptive translations. These tools remove barriers, fostering inclusion in daily interactions.

Everyday accommodations are tangible proof that an organization wants its employees to be more than just workers—it wants them to belong. When you make sure that no single day poses an undue hurdle to someone's success or sense of worth, you uphold the very essence of inclusion to say, "You are valuable here, exactly as you are."

CHALLENGES AND PITFALLS

While AI offers compelling ways to create a workplace of belonging, it also presents challenges that can undermine those very aims. Remaining attentive to these pitfalls helps you deploy AI responsibly and sustainably.

Data Bias and Underrepresentation

Historically marginalized groups might be missing or misrepresented in the data fueling AI. Algorithms trained on incomplete or skewed data might erroneously perpetuate stereotypes, such as associating leadership qualities with a narrow demographic. Vigilance requires ongoing data audits, collaboration with diverse stakeholders, and iterative model improvements so that daily AI outputs do not exclude or diminish anyone's contributions.

Black Box Algorithms and Lack of Transparency

Many advanced AI models lack explainability. Leaders and employees alike can feel uneasy if they don't understand how AI-generated recommendations—whether for promotions, scheduling, or workload distribution—are derived. A sense of mystery can erode trust, negating any positive gains in belonging. Striving for transparency, or selecting "explainable AI" solutions, ensures employees continue to feel respected and not merely computed upon.

Overreliance on Automation over Human Touch

Automation can streamline a host of tasks, from responding to HR queries to analyzing daily communication. Yet the risk is losing sight of the essential human dimension. Leaders can't delegate all critical conversations to chatbots or let AI dominate performance feedback. Genuine belonging thrives on empathy, care, and nuanced understanding—elements that require a personal, relational approach.

Ethical and Privacy Concerns

AI that monitors conversations, tracks meeting attendance, or analyzes emotional cues verge into the realm of personal privacy. Employees who feel they are under constant digital surveillance might withdraw rather than engage, especially if they don't see a clear benefit. Ethical governance, transparency about data usage, and explicit consent are crucial to fostering trust and ensuring AI is seen as a supportive ally rather than an intrusive monitor.

The company I referenced at the beginning of this chapter is well aware of concerns employees might have about privacy when they engage the in-house assistant. The tool does not "remember" any conversations and does not retain any records.

Legal and Regulatory Complexities

Compliance with antidiscrimination and privacy laws becomes more complicated when AI is involved in decisions that affect employees' careers and well-being. Leaders need to stay up-to-date on emerging regulations, ensuring that AI integrations don't inadvertently place their organizations at legal risk. Collaborating with legal counsel, IT, and HR from the outset can avert complications that damage both trust and reputations.

Identifying these challenges in advance empowers leaders to build guardrails around AI usage. When you cultivate robust oversight mechanisms, remain transparent, and maintain the "human in the loop," you preserve the integrity of an inclusive culture. AI can be a catalyst for belonging only if its application aligns with organizational values that respect and honor every individual.

GOVERNANCE CONSIDERATIONS

As AI becomes more embedded in decision-making, organizations must establish governance frameworks that balance efficiency with ethics, fairness, and accountability.

The core governance question for leaders using AI in inclusion efforts is:

> *Does AI reinforce our values of belonging, or does it unintentionally exclude?*

To ensure AI aligns with ethical leadership, organizations should adopt three key governance principles:

1. Fairness and Bias Monitoring

AI should enhance inclusion—not reinforce biases. Leaders must ensure that AI-driven hiring, performance evaluations, and sentiment analysis tools are:

✓ Regularly audited for bias
✓ Trained on diverse, representative data
✓ Reviewed by human decision-makers before final actions are taken

For example, if an AI-driven résumé screening tool consistently favors candidates from certain universities, it might be filtering out diverse talent pools. A governance framework ensures these biases are caught and corrected before AI decisions impact hiring outcomes.

2. Transparency and Explainability

Employees should understand how AI influences workplace decisions. Leaders must communicate:

✓ What data AI is analyzing
✓ How AI-generated recommendations are used
✓ Where human oversight is applied in decision-making

For example, an AI-driven promotion prediction model might suggest certain employees for advancement. If the model's decision-making process is unclear, employees may lose trust in leadership's commitment to fairness. Transparency ensures AI is seen as an enhancement, not an invisible gatekeeper.

3. Ethical Data Usage and Privacy Protection

Leaders must strike a balance between data-driven insights and individual privacy. AI-powered sentiment tracking and behavioral-analysis tools can be invasive if employees feel constantly monitored. To uphold trust, governance policies should ensure:

✓ Employees opt in to AI-driven workplace analytics
✓ AI tools don't track personal conversations without consent
✓ There are clear limits on how employee data is stored and used

For example, if AI is monitoring workplace chat sentiment, leaders should explicitly communicate: "Our AI tool aggregates trends in workplace discussions to improve engagement strategies. It does not track or retain individual conversations."

By embedding fairness, transparency, and privacy protections into AI governance, leaders set a strong ethical foundation, ensuring AI is used as a support tool for inclusion rather than a replacement for human leadership.

EVERYDAY INCLUSIVE INTERACTIONS USING AI

Bringing AI into the daily fabric of your organization calls for careful planning, collaboration, and a willingness to adapt. By approaching AI as a resource that amplifies human connection rather than replaces it, you set a strong foundation:

• Clarify your inclusion objectives: Define how you want employees to feel seen, heard, and valued. Then consider which AI tools specifically support these goals. Perhaps you need an AI chatbot that

guides managers in offering frequent recognition
or an NLP tool that identifies imbalanced participation in team meetings. Clarity ensures that
your AI investments track directly to meaningful
improvements in belonging.

+ Start small and iterate: Piloting a narrow-use
  case—like sentiment analysis on team chats—
  allows you to experiment without overwhelming
  employees or risking large-scale cultural disruption. Gather feedback not only on the tool's technical performance but also on how well it fosters
  positive, daily interactions. Refine accordingly
  and gradually expand.

+ Engage a diverse implementation team: Build
  a cross-functional coalition that includes tech
  experts, HR leaders, legal advisors, and employee-
  resource-group representatives. These varied
  perspectives help spot potential biases or cultural
  issues early on. Moreover, employees are more
  likely to trust and adopt AI initiatives if they see
  that peers who share their background or role
  helped shape the process.

+ Champion the human-AI partnership: Emphasize
  in communications and training sessions that AI
  is a supportive ally designed to augment human
  decision-making. Encourage managers to view AI
  outputs as starting points for deeper, empathetic
  conversations with team members. Reinforce
  that an employee's sense of belonging ultimately
  depends on human relationships, not algorithms.

+ Monitor, evaluate, and communicate results:
  Track key metrics like improved retention,
  increased peer recognition, or higher satisfaction with daily touchpoints. Share successes and

lessons learned broadly. If an inclusion initiative hits a roadblock—say, a tool surfaces biases you didn't anticipate—communicate transparently and outline the steps to remediate. This level of honesty cultivates trust and shared accountability.

By rolling out AI thoughtfully and fostering consistent two-way communication, you create an environment where technology enhances daily expressions of empathy, gratitude, and unity, rather than overshadowing them.

THE HUMAN FACTOR: EMPATHY AND EVERYDAY CONNECTION

No matter how sophisticated AI becomes, it cannot replicate the warmth of a personal gesture—such as a meaningful thank-you, an encouraging note, or an earnest question about someone's well-being. Inclusion is ultimately about relationships and about forming a community where each person's individuality is celebrated and their need for connection is met.

Balancing Automation with Personal Touch

Automation can help leaders remember birthdays, work anniversaries, or achievements. Yet a one-line email from an automated system pales when compared to a personal note that references a recent conversation or project. A leader might begin with an AI reminder—"Maria's one-year work anniversary is today"—but then follow up with a heartfelt, individualized message. That blend of efficiency and human authenticity is what drives home "I see you, and I appreciate you."

The Role of Storytelling and Listening Sessions

While AI can highlight broad trends, it can't capture the intricacies of individual stories unless leaders make space for them. Hosting listening circles or one-on-one check-ins allows employees to share personal experiences that shape their sense of belonging. AI might indicate rising stress levels in a department, prompting a leader to create an open forum. But the real connection happens in the ensuing dialogue, where employees feel genuinely heard and validated.

Recognizing Unique Strengths Daily

An environment of belonging blossoms when leaders regularly highlight the gifts each person brings—be it creativity, resilience, or technical expertise. AI can track achievements, but it's the daily words of appreciation that count. When employees feel their contributions are noticed, they become more open, collaborative, and motivated to grow.

Building Trust in a Hybrid or Remote World

As remote and hybrid work arrangements become the norm, many everyday interactions shift online. Leaders can harness AI tools to maintain a sense of closeness. Video calls might include real-time captioning or language translation, enabling colleagues from different backgrounds to connect more easily. Virtual coffee chats could be automatically scheduled to ensure employees in different geographies still get to know one another in casual settings. These small gestures, facilitated by AI, become a means of sustaining genuine community connections across distances.

People experience inclusion when leaders consistently express empathy, respect, and care. AI can provide the data to guide these choices, the nudges to remind us, and the analyses to help us improve. AI is a tool, but inclusion is a leadership practice. Pairing technology with intention enables leaders to build workplaces where every individual is seen, heard, and valued. It's our capacity as human beings—our willingness to listen, adapt, and love—that ultimately grants authenticity to the concept of "belonging."

CHAPTER NINE SUMMARY

THREE KEY POINTS

1. AI is developing faster than any previous technological advancement before it, which means we have to adapt quickly.

2. Understanding how AI works and what it can do is the first step toward harnessing its potential.

3. If we remain open and curious, we can try experiments such as thought partnership or brainstorming on questions about how to be more inclusionable as leaders.

THREE REFLECTIVE QUESTIONS

1. Which daily interactions in my organization represent the greatest opportunity for using AI to help employees feel seen, heard, and appreciated?

2. How can I maintain a balance between data-driven insights and meaningful human connection in a hybrid or tech-centric environment?

3. Who in the organization can I invite—across departments and demographic groups—to provide feedback and cocreate AI initiatives that truly embody belonging?

THREE ACTIONS YOU CAN TAKE

1. Daily moments of appreciation: Identify a small AI-driven nudge system or set up automatic reminders to encourage managers to share authentic words of gratitude or praise each day.

2. Listening circles informed by AI insights: Use AI to pinpoint a department or team that may be experiencing lower engagement or feeling overlooked. Organize a listening circle where employees can openly discuss challenges, share stories, and brainstorm ways to improve their sense of community.

3. Set up an inclusion buddy program: Use AI-based organizational-network analysis or sentiment data to identify employees who might be isolated—such as new hires or remote workers. Pair these individuals with experienced team members or "inclusion buddies." This approach helps them form connections and signals that the organization prioritizes belonging from the moment they arrive.

CHAPTER TEN

Commitment as a Catalyst

Until one is committed, there is hesitancy, the chance to draw back, always ineffectiveness. Concerning all acts of initiative (and creation), there is one elementary truth, the ignorance of which kills countless ideas and splendid plans: that the moment one definitely commits oneself, then providence moves too.

All sorts of things occur to help one that would never otherwise have occurred. A whole stream of events issues from the decision, raising in one's favor all manner of unforeseen incidents and meetings and material assistance, which no man could have dreamt would have come his way.

I have learned a deep respect for one of Goethe's couplets: "Whatever you can do or dream you can, begin it. Boldness has genius, power, and magic in it."

—William Hutchison Murray, *The Scottish Himalayan Expedition*, 1951[1]

I cannot remember when I first came across this quote, but I know it was a long time ago. It affected me deeply, and it's been a guiding light for me ever since. I was inspired, in part because I realized I had a means of deciding when and to what I would commit. I only wish I had come across it earlier in life, as I might've made different choices. I don't lack opportunities to commit, quite the opposite—I'm a person who sees possibility in countless paths. Sometimes those paths have been dead ends; at other times they petered or dropped precipitously out of sight. Twice I jumped anyway, assuming a soft-enough landing, and got banged up badly but survived. Once, I put the gears in reverse and retraced my path. I was shaken but proud of myself for backing down instead of bullishly continuing on.

What I learned is that I can experiment with or try out something without giving full commitment, instead holding back and testing the waters. But once I commit, the only way to go is wholehearted and all in. I have experienced confusion, grief, frustration, joy, peace, and deep fulfillment. I could tell you all about the foolish mistakes I've made, but what I would most like you to know is that I took risks; I sometimes stepped out in spite of no agreement or little support, and I learned. I am still learning. And at this stage of life, I want to learn in community with others. Writing this book has been the highest honor of my career, and much more than that, it helps fulfill my life's purpose: "I inspire others to see their own magnificence and to bring it into the world in ways that work for them."

I wrote that statement in 1985 (thank you, my beloved Martin Rutte), and it has remained the same since. I've changed, grown, and had moments of pure joy and times of failure, but I've never strayed from it. To be an inclusionable leader is an act of magnificence. It takes courage, inspiration, and perspiration. It can also be a lonely endeavor, especially if you think you may be the only person around you paying attention to these actions. All the people I interviewed were from the same company, and they didn't know what the others were doing. They volunteered to talk with me based on an email sent to a few thousand people. When I began to write this book, I interviewed people from all over the world, some new contacts and some old friends or acquaintances. In every instance, I was moved by the reflections, ideas, beliefs, and actions people had taken or things they observed. I was eager to share their stories more broadly. This is where my thinking has evolved and where community comes in.

A question I was asked as I started writing is, What do I want people to do as a result of reading my book? Of course I wanted people to actually use it and do something with it, such as experimenting with the questions and actions. Now I think it's more than that. I thought it would be enough to put this book out into the world and know that somewhere, someplace, at least a few people are applying what they learn, in a way that's fulfilling for them and that makes a difference. That would satisfy my life's purpose, wouldn't it? Yes, except that . . .

It's one thing for anyone to take in what I share and reflect on it. It's another thing for you to develop your own voice and your own practice for inclusion. Even better would be for you to contribute that voice to the world, to see that we're all grappling with similar issues of wanting to contribute, to be seen and appreciated, and to belong to something. We all have a purpose, and we want to make a difference, to matter. And to feel good and fulfilled about it.

I now declare that we can learn from each other in a community. We can spend our whole lives striving to be an effective and successful leader, but are we ever really finished? Is there ever a point where we can say, "Great, mission accomplished! We are good now"? Can we support, celebrate, and build upon each other's successes? Is being inclusionable scalable? I think it is, and to do that, I need people who are willing to engage.

And that's my request to you. In these tumultuous times

of uncertainty, fear, change, and confusion, it seems appropriate and necessary. Connect with me, and let's build a community of inclusion together. You can reach me at christine@inclusionable.com or on LinkedIn at https://linkedin.com/in/christinebarnes.

As with everything else in this book, here are a few perspectives to keep in mind as you move forward:

- **Stay curious:** Keep reflecting on your own biases and assumptions. Growth is a lifelong process.
- **Celebrate progress:** When you or others make strides toward inclusion, pause and appreciate it. It builds momentum.
- **Get feedback:** After trying something new, check in with others. Feedback gives you insight so you can refine, expand, or scale what's working.
- **Keep communicating:** Connect with others doing similar work. Share stories, metrics, and lessons learned. Keep the inspiration going.

YOUR CALL TO ACTION

Throughout this book, I've shared data, stories, and suggestions for things you can do to become a more inclusive and effective leader. Only you know how much (or how little) you might need to change to do so. For me, commitment is the cornerstone of any meaningful change. For leaders seeking to embrace inclusion and transform their organizations, the commitment quote serves as both a challenge and a guidepost. To be an inclusive leader is not to dabble in initiatives or to rest on policies alone. It is to recognize that you are accountable, to believe that you are able to be inclusive. Then comes the work of embedding inclusion into the fabric of leadership and daily operations. This work requires consistent, courageous effort—an unshakable commitment to act, reflect, and improve.

The summary below serves as both a reflection and a launchpad—an invitation to take what you've learned and translate it into meaningful, lasting action. Each paragraph revisits a key insight from the chapter, followed by one sure step you can take to move from awareness to impact. You may think of other actions, too, but I invite you to think of this as your inclusion catalyst—a set of focused, tangible ways to turn commitment into practice, ensuring that inclusion is not just an idea you support but a leadership approach you embody every day.

Introduction: Hidden Heroes

What I said: Inclusion is an untapped opportunity and an underused strategy leaders can tap into to authentically motivate employees, which in turn can improve business results. I believe it lies within everyone who is a leader to do this. And sometimes we find heroes who can champion inclusion even if we aren't looking for them.

Your catalyst for inclusion: Commit to looking around you, beginning today, for opportunities to exercise your superpower of inclusion. If you find it difficult, notice who around you seems to be getting on with it. These are your hidden heroes.

Chapter One: How Did We Get Here?

What I said: While laws like the Civil Rights Act of 1964 and affirmative action provided the initial framework for equality, they also highlighted the complexity of translating legal mandates into practical workplace practices. Inclusion came about much later and is now understood as something that leaders can influence regardless of what the broader organization is doing. Inclusion is harder to see and measure.

Your catalyst for inclusion: Understand the distinction between diversity and inclusion for you. If it's difficult to articulate the differences between the two, that's okay! You are paying attention, and you are ready to go deeper into this important step in your journey.

Chapter Two: Know Yourself

What I said: As leaders, we cannot effectively drive inclusion without first understanding our own identities, biases, and privileges. I described different levels of knowledge to help move from knowing about inclusion to actively practicing it and reflecting on how we can continuously improve.

Your catalyst for inclusion: Reflect on what you could do more or less of to demonstrate inclusionable behavior. Pick one thing and try it for thirty days, then reflect again.

Chapter Three: Know Your Team

What I said: Leaders can foster inclusion at every stage of a team's development—forming, storming, norming, performing, and adjourning. A leader's ability to create an inclusive team environment is directly linked to employee engagement, innovation, and performance.

Your catalyst for inclusion: Identify what stage your team is at, and involve team members in inclusive actions such as creating or revising a charter of agreements for how work is done.

Chapter Four: Know Your Organization

What I said: I asked you to expand beyond knowing yourself and your team to realize you are part of a complex system. I explained two pillars of support. The Star Model provides the systems-level blueprint, while Edgar Schein's insights framework ensures these systems are rooted in authentic cultural change.

Your catalyst for inclusion: Observe and diagnose the tangible and intangible elements of your own organization. Get curious about how the organization's systems influence the culture.

Chapter Five: Know the Business Problem

What I said: It's critical to understand the business problem you're trying to solve, including identifying gaps and assessing root causes, before turning to actions that involve inclusion. Jumping to solutions immediately upon hearing of a problem is almost certain to fail.

Your catalyst for inclusion: Stop and take a breath. Confirm that you and anyone else involved know the problem, the gaps, and the root causes before you decide on any solutions. This is true for any business problem, but especially for addressing concerns with inclusive behavior.

Chapter Six: When "Good" Is Better Than "Best"

What I said: Modeling inclusive leadership does not take grand, complicated gestures or training. Leaders can influence team culture positively by demonstrating inclusive behaviors, actively seeking input, and recognizing contributions, which fosters trust and engagement. And all these things can be done daily and become good habits over time.

Your catalyst for inclusion: Pick one topic you need to take action on, and before you implement a solution, seek out at least two other people whose input you don't normally seek but who have some knowledge of, interest in, or responsibility in this area. Get their input and thank them for meeting with you, even if you don't do anything different as a result.

Chapter Seven: Implement Inclusion for Continuous Improvement

What I said: I described the Plan-Do-Check-Act (PDCA) cycle as a practical framework for embedding inclusion into everyday leadership. This method is used to ensure continuous improvement in business, and I want very much for you to have something practical you can apply.

Your catalyst for inclusion: Set a personal inclusion target for yourself, such as ensuring every member of your team understands what you value about their contribution. This ensures you begin at the beginning, with the "plan" step.

Chapter Eight: You Are Not Alone: Support for Inclusionable Leaders

What I said: I highlighted the value and the importance of working with professionals who can support your inclusion journey but who you might not think of immediately. For example, organization effectiveness experts can help you set key performance indicators (KPIs) to enable your inclusion efforts.

Your catalyst for inclusion: Commit to reaching out this week to someone in your network who can be an ally for you. Give yourself bonus points if it's someone you haven't yet discussed inclusion with.

Chapter Nine: Is Artificial Intelligence Inclusive?

What I said: AI has the potential to amplify both opportunities and risks for inclusion, depending on how it's designed and implemented. For example, AI can suggest actions that enhance inclusion, but with the risks of algorithmic bias, poorly designed AI can hamper progress or worse.

Your catalyst for inclusion: Learn about AI if you have yet to do so; free classes abound. If you're familiar with it, experiment. It can be a thought-provoking, idea-generating assistant, but it should never replace your own ethical and thoughtful behaviors.

BOOK SUMMARY

THREE KEY POINTS

1. Inclusion is an enabler of diversity. It requires self-awareness and commitment to understand how it can enhance your leadership. Address systemic inequities at every level of leadership.

2. If you're a leader, you are accountable for creating an environment where each person knows they are valued and that they belong. Hard stop. It's not the job of human resources, the company CEO, or the DEI person. That said, you are able to be that inclusive leader. It does not require special training or certification or years and years of practice. It takes one action, one day at a time, to build that environment.

3. Inclusionable leadership is both a business strategy and a direct path to employee engagement.

THREE REFLECTIVE QUESTIONS

1. How inclusive was I today?

2. What is one sure thing I can commit to after reading this book?

3. What is possible from here?

THREE ACTIONS YOU CAN TAKE

1. Conduct a personal audit of your leadership practices, identifying areas where you can enhance inclusion.

2. Start now. Start big or small; it doesn't matter. Just start.

3. Give yourself grace and space to keep going, to make mistakes, to fall back, and to regroup. It will be worth it.

ACKNOWLEDGMENTS

A stellar cast of characters made this book possible, at different stages of the process and for different reasons.

Karen Williams, of Librotas.com skillfully guided me through the transition from academic to narrative writing and didn't even blink when I naively said I thought it would be "pretty easy" to turn my doctoral dissertation into a book. It wasn't easy at all! Karen's templates, tools, and encouragement helped me get my manuscript ready to submit to publishers.

One of Karen's many excellent recommendations was to interview leaders and those who support them about what would make them pick up a book about inclusion. In doing so, I was struck by what a diverse community I have. Colleagues from multiple industries, organizations, and professions provided insights that strengthened my writing. Many thanks to **Doug Smith III; Beverly Kaye; Beverley Wright; Debbie Page; Victoria Shiroma Wilson, EdD; Newton Cheng; Deary Duffie; Diontrey Thompson, EdD; Brent Obleton, EdD; Christopher Riddick, EdD;** and **Amy Elizabeth Fox** for being so generous with your time and support.

Gabriel Powell; Jerry Washington, EdD; and **Sam Isaacson** influenced the chapter on artificial intelligence (AI) and inclusion. I realized how basic my own understanding was after learning of their contributions to a field that's traveling at light speed through society, leaving many of us scrambling to keep up.

It takes a special kind of colleague to willingly say yes when asked to do not one but two things. I owe a huge debt to **Andrew Chandler** and **Germain St-Denis**, who not only patiently answered my interview questions but also read a first draft before I submitted it to publishers.

Susan Matsushima; Julia Jim, EdD; and **Pamela Kelly, EdD** also read the first draft and provided many excellent suggestions.

Throughout every stage of writing this book, I have felt seen and appreciated by others. No matter how busy they were, how long it had been since we last spoke, or how new our acquaintance, everyone I reached out to engaged with me in meaningful conversations about inclusion.

May these connections continue, deepen, and expand.

RESOURCES

Throughout this book, I've shared tools and templates that have helped me during more than thirty years in organization development, coaching, and change leadership. Here you'll find more details about those resources, along with others that can support your team at different stages of development. This isn't an exhaustive list—just a collection of things I've found genuinely helpful.

What matters most is what works for *you*. As you explore these resources, you might find some familiar favorites or discover something new to try.

TOOLS THAT HELP YOU KNOW YOURSELF AND OTHERS

These tools are helpful for understanding individual styles, preferences, and motivations, which is foundational to inclusion.

CliftonStrengths
(certified facilitator not required but recommended)

- *Purpose:* Identifies individual talents and strengths.
- *Why it's useful:* Highlights what each person naturally does best and how to build partnerships that maximize team impact.

Myers-Briggs Type Indicator (MBTI)
(certified facilitator required)

- *Purpose:* Explores personality preferences based on Jungian psychology.
- *Why it's useful:* Helps team members understand and appreciate how others think, plan, and make decisions.

Enneagram
(certified facilitator not required but recommended)

- *Purpose:* Reveals core motivations and emotional patterns across nine personality types.
- *Why it's useful:* Encourages self-awareness and compassion, especially around how people respond to stress and growth.

The Big Five Personality Test
(certified facilitator not required but recommended)

- *Purpose:* Measures personality along five major dimensions: openness, conscientiousness, extraversion, agreeableness, and neuroticism.
- *Why it's useful:* Offers a research-backed, straightforward view of personality that helps explain interpersonal dynamics.

Hogan Personality Inventory (HPI)
(certified facilitator required)

- *Purpose:* Predicts job performance by assessing personality traits.

- *Why it's useful:* Especially helpful for leadership development and succession planning.

TOOLS THAT SUPPORT TEAM EFFECTIVENESS

These tools are ideal when the focus is on group dynamics, team trust, and collaboration.

The Five Behaviors of a Cohesive Team
(certified facilitator not required but recommended)

- *Purpose:* Builds team trust, encourages healthy conflict, and drives commitment, accountability, and results.
- *Why it's useful:* A full-team lens that diagnoses barriers to group success.

Team Emotional Intelligence (EI) Survey
(certified facilitator not required but recommended)

- *Purpose:* Evaluates how effectively a team uses emotional intelligence.
- *Why it's useful:* Brings awareness to emotional dynamics that can make or break collaboration.

Leadership Circle Profile
(certified facilitator required)

- *Purpose:* Measures leadership effectiveness through reactive and creative tendencies.
- *Why it's useful:* Integrates individual and collective insight for leadership teams striving for growth and transformation.

TOOLS THAT ADDRESS COMMUNICATION AND CONFLICT

These are especially valuable when teams need to better understand how they interact under pressure.

DiSC Assessment
(certified facilitator not required but recommended)

- *Purpose:* Measures communication and behavioral preferences.
- *Why it's useful:* Offers a common language for navigating different communication styles.

Thomas-Kilmann Conflict Mode Instrument (TKI)
(certified facilitator not required but recommended)

- *Purpose:* Assesses how individuals approach conflict across five modes: competing, collaborating, compromising, avoiding, and accommodating.
- *Why it's useful:* Helps teams develop strategies to manage disagreement productively.

Herrmann Brain Dominance Instrument (HBDI)
(certified facilitator required)

- *Purpose:* Identifies thinking preferences across four quadrants: analytical, practical, relational, and experimental.
- *Why it's useful:* A practical tool for improving collaboration, problem-solving, and communication.

WRAPPING UP

You don't need to use all these tools to be an inclusive leader—
you just need the ones that give you insight, spark conversation, or help your team grow together. Pick what fits your
context, experiment a little, and trust your judgment. The goal
isn't perfection—it's awareness, connection, and progress.

NOTES

CHAPTER ONE: HOW DID WE GET HERE?

1   Bernardo M. Ferdman, "The Practice of Inclusion in Diverse Organizations: Toward a Systematic and Inclusive Framework," in *Diversity at Work: The Practice of Inclusion*, ed. Bernardo M. Ferdman, assoc. ed. Barbara R. Deane (Jossey-Bass, 2014), 3–54.

2   Michàlle E. Mor Barak, *Managing Diversity: Toward a Globally Inclusive Workplace*, 5th ed. (SAGE Publications, 2022), xv.

3   A. V. Korkmaz et al., "About and Beyond Leading Uniqueness and Belongingness: A Systematic Review of Inclusive Leadership Research," *Human Resources Management Review* 32, no. 4 (2022): article 100894.

4   Ken Follett, *The Pillars of the Earth* (William Morrow, 1989).

5   R. Roosevelt Thomas, Jr. "Managing Diversity: A Conceptual Framework," in *Diversity in the Workplace: Human Resources Initiatives* (Guildford Press, 1992), 306–317.

6   Mor Barak, *Managing Diversity*, 12–15.

7   Henri Tajfel, *Social Identity and Intergroup Relations* (Cambridge University Press, 1982), 15–40.

8   Ingrid M. Nembhard and Amy C. Edmondson, "Making It Safe: The Effects of Leader Inclusiveness and Professional Status on Psychological Safety and Improvement Efforts in Health Care Teams," *Journal of Organizational Behavior* 27, no. 7 (2006): 941–966.

9   Ferdman, *Diversity at Work*, 8.

10 Greg Filbeck et al., "Does Diversity Improve Profits and Shareholder Returns? Evidence from Top Rated Companies for Diversity by DiversityInc," *Advances in Accounting* 37 (2017): 94–102.

11 US Census Bureau, "HINC-02. Age of Householder– Households, by Total Money Income, Type of Household, Race and Hispanic Origin of Householder: 2022," *Current Population Survey, 2023 Annual Social and Economic Supplement*, accessed March 15, 2025, https://www .census.gov/data/tables/time-series/demo/income -poverty/cps-hinc/hinc-02.html.

12 Lynn M. Shore et al., "Inclusion and Diversity in Work Groups: A Review and Model for Future Research," *Journal of Management* 37, no. 4 (2011): 1,262–1,289.

13 Sara Harrison, "Five Years of Tech Diversity Reports—and Little Progress," *Wired.com*, October 1, 2019, https:// www.wired.com/story/five-years-tech-diversity-reports -little-progress/.

14 Rob Price, "Facebook's Annual Diversity Report Shows It's Making Little Headway on Boosting Its Numbers of Black Employees," *Business Insider*, July 15, 2020, https://www .businessinsider.com/facebook-2020-diversity-report -slow-progress-black-employees-2020-7.

15 US Equal Employment Opportunity Commission (EEOC), *Diversity in High Tech* (EEOC, 2014), accessed March 15, 2025, https://www.eeoc.gov/sites/default/files /migrated_files/eeoc/statistics/reports/hightech/diversity -in-high-tech-report.pdf.

16 Allison Scott et al., "Tech Leavers Study: A First-of-Its- Kind Analysis of Why People Voluntarily Left Jobs in Tech," Kapor Center for Social Impact, April 27, 2017, https://kaporcenter.org/the-2017-tech-leavers-study.

17 Christopher G. Worley et al., *The Agility Factor: Building Adaptable Organizations for Superior Performance* (Jossey-Bass, 2014).

CHAPTER TWO: KNOW YOURSELF

1 Steve Adubato, *Lessons in Leadership* (Rutgers University Press, 2016), 26.
2 Lorin W. Anderson and David R. Krathwohl, eds., *A Taxonomy for Learning, Teaching, and Assessing: A Revision of Bloom's Taxonomy of Educational Objectives* (Longman, 2001), 46–48.
3 Stephen R. Covey, *The 7 Habits of Highly Effective People* (Simon & Schuster, 1989).

CHAPTER THREE: KNOW YOUR TEAM

1 Patrick Lencioni, *The Five Dysfunctions of a Team: A Leadership Fable* (Jossey-Bass, 2002), vii.
2 Patrick Lencioni, *Overcoming the Five Dysfunctions of a Team: A Field Guide for Leaders, Managers, and Facilitators* (Jossey-Bass, 2005), 3.
3 DovileMi, *Bruce Tuckman's Stages of Team Development*, Wikimedia Commons, accessed February 9, 2025, https://commons.wikimedia.org/wiki/File:Team-development -stages.png, licensed under CC BY-SA 4.0.
4 Shore et al., "Inclusion and Diversity in Work Groups," 1,265.
5 Amy C. Edmondson, "Psychological Safety and Learning Behavior in Work Teams," *Administrative Science Quarterly* 44, no. 2 (1999): 350–383.

6   Edmondson, "Psychological Safety," 354.

7   Peter G. Northouse, *Introduction to Leadership: Concepts and Practice*, 6th ed. (SAGE Publications, 2025), 302–304.

8   Korkmaz et al., "About and Beyond Leading Uniqueness and Belongingness."

9   Sundiatu Dixon-Fyle et al., "Diversity Wins: How Inclusion Matters," McKinsey & Company, May 2020, https://www.mckinsey.com/featured-insights/diversity -and-inclusion/diversity-wins-how-inclusion-matters.

10   Lencioni, *Five Dysfunctions of a Team*, 188.

11   Amy C. Edmondson, *Teaming: How Organizations Learn, Innovate, and Compete in the Knowledge Economy* (Jossey-Bass, 2012), 4.

12   Pilar Gallegos, "The Work of Inclusive Leadership," in *Diversity at Work: The Practice of Inclusion*, ed. Bernardo M. Ferdman, assoc. ed. Barbara R. Deane (Jossey-Bass, 2014), 177–202.

13   Pamela Duke et al., "Preserving Third-Year Medical Students' Empathy and Enhancing Self-Reflection Using Small Group 'Virtual Hangout' Technology," *Medical Teacher* 37, no. 6 (2014): 566–571, https://doi.org/10.3109 /0142159X.2014.956057.

14   Wikipedia, "Perspective-taking," last modified April 21, 2024, accessed February 15, 2025, https://en.wikipedia .org/wiki/Perspective-taking.

15   Duke et al., "Preserving Third-Year Medical Students' Empathy," 568.

16   J. A. Joireman et al., "Empathy and the Self-Absorption Paradox: Support for the Distinction Between Self-Rumination and Self-Reflection," *Self and Identity* 1, no. 1 (2002): 53–65, https://doi.org/10.1080 /152988602317232803.

17 Wikipedia, "Motivation," last modified March 8, 2025, accessed March 15, 2025, https://en.wikipedia.org/wiki/Motivation.

CHAPTER FOUR: KNOW YOUR ORGANIZATION

1 Amy E. Randel et al., "Inclusive Leadership: Realizing Positive Outcomes Through Belongingness and Being Valued for Uniqueness," *Human Resources Management Review* 28, no. 2 (2018): 190–203, https://doi.org/10.1016/j.hrmr.2017.07.002.

2 Jay R. Galbraith, The Star Model™, accessed September 13, 2025, https://jaygalbraith.com.

3 Jay Galbraith, Diane Downey and Amy Kates, *Designing Dynamic Organizations: A Hands-On Guide for Leaders at All Levels*, (AMACOM 2002).

4 Beverly Kaye and Sharon Jordan-Evans, *Hello Stay Interviews, Goodbye Talent Loss: A Manager's Playbook* (Berrett-Koehler Publishers, 2015).

5 Edgar H. Schein, *Organizational Culture and Leadership*, 3rd ed. (Jossey-Bass, 2004), 17.

6 Schein, *Organizational Culture and Leadership*, 23–31.

7 Tim Kuppler, "Culture Fundamentals—9 Important Insights from Edgar Schein," *Culture University*, September 10, 2014, https://rpgroup.org/Portals/0/Documents/Events/SummerInstitute/SI2018/2018_Past_Resources/Pre-InstituteReadings/CultureFundamentals.pdf?ver=2020-02-22-082348-750.

8 Robert Rueda, *The 3 Dimensions of Improving Student Performance: Finding the Right Solutions to the Right Problems* (Teachers College Press, 2011), 54.

CHAPTER FIVE: KNOW THE BUSINESS PROBLEM

1   Kimberlé Crenshaw, "The Urgency of Intersectionality,"
    TED, video, 18:39, October 2016, YouTube, https://www
    .ted.com/talks/kimberle_crenshaw_the_urgency_of
    _intersectionality.
2   Richard E. Clark and Fred Estes, *Turning Research into
    Results: A Guide to Selecting the Right Performance
    Solutions* (Information Age Publishing, 2008), 44.

CHAPTER SIX: WHEN "GOOD" IS BETTER THAN "BEST"

1   Mary-Frances Winters, "From Diversity to Inclusion: An
    Inclusion Equation," in *Diversity at Work: The Practice of
    Inclusion*, ed. Bernardo M. Ferdman, assoc. ed. Barbara R.
    Deane (Jossey-Bass, 2014), 205–228.
2   Satya Nadella, *Hit Refresh: The Quest to Rediscover
    Microsoft's Soul and Imagine a Better Future for Everyone*
    (Harper Business, 2017).
3   Gallegos, "The Work of Inclusive Leadership," 182–188.
4   Randel et al., "Inclusive Leadership," 190.
5   D. S. Wang and C. C. Hsieh, "The Effect of Authentic
    Leadership on Employee Trust and Employee
    Engagement," *Social Behavior and Personality: An
    International Journal* 41, no. 4 (2013): 613–624.
6   Shore et al., "Inclusion and Diversity in Work Groups," 1,265.
7   Jean-Pierre Brun and Ninon Dugas, "An Analysis of
    Employee Recognition: Perspectives on Human Resources
    Practices," *The International Journal of Human Resource
    Management* 19, no. 4 (2008): 716–730, https://doi.org
    /10.1080/09585190801953723.
8   K. C. Brimhall, "Inclusion Is Important . . . But How Do

I Include? Examining the Effects of Leader Engagement on Inclusion, Innovation, Job Satisfaction, and Perceived Quality of Care in a Diverse Nonprofit Health Care Organization," *Nonprofit and Voluntary Sector Quarterly* 48, no. 4 (2019): 716–737, https://doi.org/10.1177 /0899764019829834.

9   "How Salesforce Builds Meaningful Employee Experiences—Without Return-to-Office Mandates," Salesforce.com, September 15, 2022, https://www .salesforce.com/news/stories/how-salesforce-builds -meaningful-employee-experiences/.

10 Amy E. Randel et al., "Leader Inclusiveness, Psychological Diversity Climate, and Helping Behaviors," *Journal of Managerial Psychology* 31, no. 1 (2016): 216–234, https:// doi.org/10.1108/JMP-04-2013-0123.

11 R. Roosevelt Thomas Jr., "Diversity Management and Affirmative Action: Past, Present and Future," paper presented at the Diversity Symposium, October 7, 2004, https://www.diversitycollegium.org/pdf2004 /2004Thomaspaper.pdf.

12 Korkmaz et al., "About and Beyond Leading Uniqueness and Belongingness."

CHAPTER SEVEN: IMPLEMENT INCLUSION FOR CONTINUOUS IMPROVEMENT

1   W. Edwards Deming, *Out of the Crisis* (MIT Press, 1986), 88–94.

2   Christoph Roser at AllAboutLean.com, *Plan, Do, Check, Act* diagram, licensed under CC BY-SA 4.0, Wikimedia Commons, accessed March 2, 2025, https://commons .wikimedia.org/wiki/File:PDCA-Loop.png.

3   James D. Kirkpatrick and Wendy Kayser Kirkpatrick, *Kirkpatrick's Four Levels of Training Evaluation* (Association for Talent Development, 2016), 20–25.
4   Clark and Estes, *Turning Research into Results*, 141.
5   Clark and Estes, *Turning Research into Results*, 151.
6   Kirkpatrick and Kirkpatrick, *Kirkpatrick's Four Levels of Training Evaluation*, 120.

CHAPTER EIGHT: YOU ARE NOT ALONE: SUPPORT FOR INCLUSIONABLE LEADERS

1   Shaneeta M. Johnson and Henry Lin, "Diversity, Equity, and Inclusion: Transparency, Measures, and Accountability," in *The SAGES Manual of Strategy and Leadership* (Springer, 2024), 701–722.
2   Ellyn Shook et al., "How Companies Can Use Employee Data Responsibly," *Harvard Business Review*, February 15, 2019, https://hbr.org/2019/02/how-companies-can-use-employee-data-responsibly.

CHAPTER TEN: COMMITMENT AS A CATALYST

1   W. H. Murray, *The Scottish Himalayan Expedition* (J. M. Dent & Sons, 1951).

ABOUT THE AUTHOR

DR. CHRISTINE BARNES is an organization development expert, executive coach, and change leader who helps executives and teams tackle complex challenges while building inclusive, innovative work environments. Her doctoral dissertation, "Inclusionary Practices of Leaders in a Biotechnology Company: A Gap Analysis," was the inspiration for this book.

www.ingramcontent.com/pod-product-compliance
Lightning Source LLC
Chambersburg PA
CBHW030504210326
41597CB00013B/787